SELF-LEARNING MANAGEMENT SERIES

VIBRANT PUBLISHERS

GRAPH MACHINE LEARNING ESSENTIALS

Introduction to graph machine learning, hands-on implementations, and applied use cases.

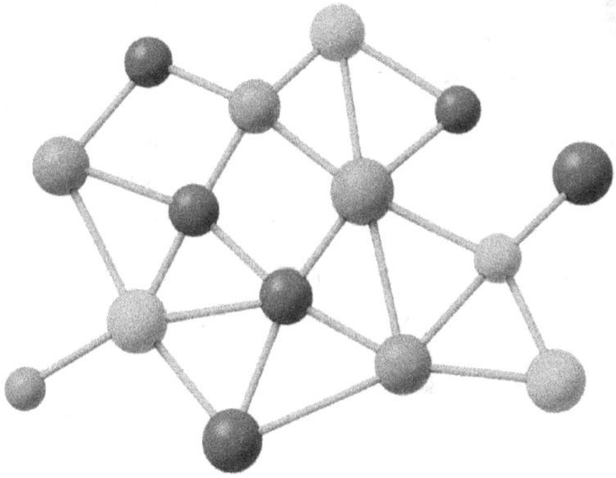

PINTU KUMAR

GRAPH MACHINE LEARNING ESSENTIALS

First Edition

Published by Vibrant Publishers LLC, USA, www.vibrantpublishers.com

Paperback ISBN 13:978-1-63651-725-4
Ebook ISBN 13: 978-1-63651-726-1
Hardback ISBN 13: 978-1-63651-727-8

Library of Congress Control Number: 2026939407

Exclusive Online Resources For You

As our valued reader, your purchase of this book includes access to exclusive online resources designed to enhance your learning experience. These resources can be downloaded from our website, www.vibrantpublishers.com, and are created to help you apply graph machine learning concepts effectively.

Online resources for this book include the following:

- **Programming Assignments through Google Colab:**
  Hands-on programming assignments have been integrated across **Chapters 2–5** that turn concepts into practice. These exercises will help you apply graph machine learning techniques, strengthen your understanding, and build real-world problem-solving skills.
- **In-text Quizzes:**
  Three interactive **quizzes** have been embedded in **Chapter 2**, accessible via QR codes, allowing you to assess understanding in real time, apply concepts, and reinforce key ideas as you progress.

How to access your online resources:

1. **Visit the website:** Go to www.vibrantpublishers.com
2. **Find your book:** Navigate to the book's product page via the "Shop" menu or by searching for the book title in the search bar.
3. **Request the resources:** Scroll down to the "Request Sample Book/Online Resource" section.

4. **Enter your details:** Enter your preferred email ID and select "Online Resource" as the resource type. Lastly, select "user type" and submit the request.
5. **Check your inbox:** The resources will be delivered directly to your email.

Alternatively, for quick access: simply scan the QR code below to go directly to the product page and request the online resources by filling in the required details.

Happy learning!

SELF-LEARNING MANAGEMENT SERIES

TITLE	PAPERBACK* ISBN
BUSINESS AND ENTREPRENEURSHIP	
BUSINESS COMMUNICATION ESSENTIALS	9781636511634
BUSINESS ETHICS ESSENTIALS	9781636513324
BUSINESS LAW ESSENTIALS	9781636511702
BUSINESS PLAN ESSENTIALS	9781636511214
BUSINESS STRATEGY ESSENTIALS	9781949395778
ENTREPRENEURSHIP ESSENTIALS	9781636511603
INTERNATIONAL BUSINESS ESSENTIALS	9781636513294
PRINCIPLES OF MANAGEMENT ESSENTIALS	9781636511542
PRINCIPLES OF MANAGEMENT ESSENTIALS (Sp.Ed)	9781636514994
THE PROFITABLE GOOD	9781636516660
COMPUTER SCIENCE AND TECHNOLOGY	
ARTIFICIAL INTELLIGENCE ESSENTIALS	9781636516387
BLOCKCHAIN ESSENTIALS	9781636513003
CYBERSECURITY ESSENTIALS	9781636514888
DATA STRUCTURES AND ALGORITHMS ESSENTIALS	9781636516325
JAVA ESSENTIALS VOLUME 1	9781636515021
JAVA ESSENTIALS VOLUME 2	9781636516561
MACHINE LEARNING ESSENTIALS	9781636513775
PYTHON ESSENTIALS	9781636512938
DATA SCIENCE FOR BUSINESS	
BUSINESS ANALYTICS ESSENTIALS	9781636514154
BUSINESS INTELLIGENCE ESSENTIALS	9781636513362
BUSINESS STATISTICS ESSENTIALS	9781636514826
DATA ANALYTICS ESSENTIALS	9781636511184
MICROSOFT POWER BI ESSENTIALS	9781636515717

*Also available in Hardback & Ebook formats

SELF-LEARNING MANAGEMENT SERIES

TITLE	PAPERBACK* ISBN
FINANCIAL LITERACY AND ECONOMICS	
COST ACCOUNTING & MANAGEMENT ESSENTIALS	9781636511030
FINANCIAL ACCOUNTING ESSENTIALS	9781636510972
FINANCIAL MANAGEMENT ESSENTIALS	9781636511009
MACROECONOMICS ESSENTIALS	9781636511818
MICROECONOMICS ESSENTIALS	9781636511153
PERSONAL FINANCE ESSENTIALS	9781636511849
PRINCIPLES OF ECONOMICS ESSENTIALS	9781636512334
HR, DIVERSITY, AND ORGANIZATIONAL SUCCESS	
DIVERSITY, EQUITY, AND INCLUSION ESSENTIALS	9781636512976
DIVERSITY IN THE WORKPLACE ESSENTIALS	9781636511122
HR ANALYTICS ESSENTIALS	9781636510347
HUMAN RESOURCE MANAGEMENT ESSENTIALS	9781949395839
LABOR RELATIONS ESSENTIALS	9781636516493
ORGANIZATIONAL BEHAVIOR ESSENTIALS	9781636512303
ORGANIZATIONAL DEVELOPMENT ESSENTIALS	9781636511481
LEADERSHIP AND PERSONAL DEVELOPMENT	
BETTER: A GUIDEBOOK TO A NEW AND IMPROVED YOU	9781636516745
DECISION MAKING ESSENTIALS	9781636510026
INCLUSIVE LEADERSHIP ESSENTIALS	9781636514765
INDIA'S ROAD TO TRANSFORMATION: WHY LEADERSHIP MATTERS	9781636512273
LEADERSHIP ESSENTIALS	9781636510316
PUBLIC SPEAKING ESSENTIALS	9781636516356
TIME MANAGEMENT ESSENTIALS	9781636511665

*Also available in Hardback & Ebook formats

SELF-LEARNING MANAGEMENT SERIES

TITLE	PAPERBACK* ISBN
MODERN MARKETING AND SALES	
BRAND MANAGEMENT ESSENTIALS	9781636515595
CONSUMER BEHAVIOR ESSENTIALS	9781636513263
DIGITAL CONSUMER BEHAVIOR ESSENTIALS	9781636516622
DIGITAL MARKETING ESSENTIALS	9781949395747
MARKETING MANAGEMENT ESSENTIALS	9781636511788
MARKET RESEARCH ESSENTIALS	9781636513744
MODERN ADVERTISING ESSENTIALS	9781636514857
SALES MANAGEMENT ESSENTIALS	9781636510743
SERVICES MARKETING ESSENTIALS	9781636511733
SOCIAL MEDIA MARKETING ESSENTIALS	9781636512181

OPERATIONS MANAGEMENT

TITLE	PAPERBACK* ISBN
AGILE ESSENTIALS	9781636516417
CONTINUOUS IMPROVEMENT ESSENTIALS	9781636516714
OPERATIONS & SUPPLY CHAIN MANAGEMENT ESSENTIALS	9781949395242
OPERATIONAL EXCELLENCE ESSENTIALS	9781636516592
PRODUCT MANAGEMENT ESSENTIALS	9781636514796
PROJECT MANAGEMENT ESSENTIALS	9781636510712
STAKEHOLDER ENGAGEMENT ESSENTIALS	9781636511511

*Also available in Hardback & Ebook formats

About the Author

Pintu Kumar is a dedicated researcher specializing in graph machine learning. He is currently pursuing a Ph.D. in the Department of Industrial Engineering & Operations Research at the Indian Institute of Technology Bombay (IIT Bombay).

Pintu holds a strong academic foundation in mathematics, having completed his B.Sc. (Hons) in Mathematics from Motilal Nehru College, University of Delhi, followed by an M.Sc. in Mathematics from IIT Jodhpur. He graduated as a Silver Medalist, a distinction awarded for academic excellence. His background reflects a deep analytical approach and a passion for solving complex problems, which naturally led him to the field of machine learning.

His research excellence has been recognized through prestigious fellowships, including the highly competitive Prime Minister's Research Fellowship (PMRF) and the CSIR Junior Research Fellowship (JRF). These awards reflect his strong commitment to advancing graph machine learning, focusing on both theoretical foundations and practical applications. He has published impactful research papers in top-tier ML and AI conferences, including ECML.

In addition to research, Pintu is actively involved in teaching and knowledge dissemination. As a teaching assistant, he has supported courses covering topics such as Machine Learning, Deep Learning, Probability, Optimization, and Python Lab. He has also contributed to the National Programme on Technology Enhanced Learning

(NPTEL) PMRF program by conducting live tutorial sessions and helping create educational content on machine learning and mathematics that has reached thousands of learners across India.

Pintu's work bridges the gap between theory and practice, focusing on making advanced graph machine learning concepts understandable and applicable. His research includes designing scalable graph neural network algorithms, solving real-world challenges like noisy graph data, and developing theoretical insights into how graph embeddings work.

This book is the result of Pintu's passion for simplifying complex ideas without losing their rigor, making graph machine learning accessible to students, researchers, and industry practitioners who want to understand and apply these techniques effectively.

What Experts Say About This Book!

Graph Machine Learning Essentials delivers a practical and technically grounded introduction to modern Graph ML, effectively connecting foundational graph concepts with real-world AI implementation workflows.

– Lucas Cabral, AI Engineer & Data Scientist

Graph Machine Learning Essentials is a compact, practical guide for engineers who want a quick start in Graph ML, covering key methods, tasks, applications, and implementation pathways. It is a valuable handbook for navigating modern graph ML concepts and real-world pipelines.

– Dymitr Nowicki, Ph.D. in Computer Science and Applied Mathematics, Selecton Technologies Inc.

A comprehensive and accessible introduction to the burgeoning field of graph machine learning (GML). Aimed at readers with a basic understanding of machine learning, the book expertly balances theory and practice, making it suitable for students, professionals, and researchers alike.

The book begins by introducing graphs as structures that model relationships between entities, highlighting their ubiquity in domains like social networks, biology, and finance. Pintu explains why traditional machine learning methods fall short for graph-structured data, setting the stage for specialized techniques like node embeddings and Graph Neural Networks (GNNs). Each chapter builds logically on the last, covering core tasks (node classification, edge prediction, graph classification), advanced architectures, and practical considerations like scalability and over-smoothing.

What Experts Say About This Book!

What sets the book apart is its practical focus. Pintu includes code snippets, programming assignments, and discussions on real-world applications—such as fraud detection, recommender systems, and drug discovery—to ensure readers can apply what they learn. The use of quizzes and examples further reinforces understanding, while appendices on machine learning basics and PyTorch Geometric make the book self-contained.

Graph Machine Learning Essentials is an invaluable guide for anyone looking to understand and apply GML, offering both the theoretical foundations and the practical tools needed to harness the power of graph-structured data.

– Wilson Yeung, Reviewer

Table of Contents

Preface

Graph Machine Learning has emerged as one of the most exciting and rapidly growing areas in both research and industry. Graph-structured data is everywhere — from social networks and recommendation systems to biological networks and supply chains. This new paradigm of learning from graphs offers powerful ways to capture complex relationships and dependencies that traditional machine learning methods struggle to handle.

When I first started exploring graph machine learning, I found that there were very few resources available that provided a clear and comprehensive introduction. While some books have appeared since then, they are mostly targeted at researchers with advanced knowledge of the field and often focus heavily on theoretical concepts without offering practical implementation guidance. On the other hand, many online tutorials provide useful code examples but lack the depth of explanation needed to understand why and how graph learning methods actually work.

This gap motivated me to write this book, a resource that builds graph machine learning from scratch. The goal has been to create a balanced guide that provides both theoretical foundations and practical implementations in a way that is approachable for a wide audience. I designed the content assuming only a basic knowledge of machine learning as a prerequisite, making it suitable for undergraduate students who have completed introductory ML courses, working professionals aiming to apply graph learning in their projects, and researchers entering the field.

Throughout this book, you will find clear explanations of key concepts such as graph construction, graph neural network fundamentals, advanced GNN architectures, and practical challenges like scalability and robustness. Each theoretical concept is accompanied by simple, hands-on examples and code snippets to help you build a solid intuition and apply what you learn in practice. Moreover, the book covers recent advancements in the field, ensuring that readers are up to date with current developments.

I hope that this book serves as both a learning companion and a practical reference, empowering readers to understand and apply graph machine learning effectively in their own work. I also encourage readers to experiment with the provided examples and explore further resources to deepen their knowledge.

Introduction to the book

Recently, ***Graph Machine Learning (Graph ML)*** has emerged as one of the most powerful and promising areas in the field of machine learning. Unlike traditional data structures such as tables or images, graph-structured data models complex relationships between entities. These relationships are central to many real-world problems, from social network analysis and recommendation systems to biological network modeling and fraud detection. As a result, graph machine learning has rapidly gained traction in both research and industry.

Why Graph Machine Learning Matters

Graphs are everywhere. A social network connects people through friendships, a molecular graph represents atoms connected by chemical bonds, and a transportation network models roads connecting cities. The challenge is that standard machine learning models often struggle to capture the relationships between two nodes (entities) of graphs. That's where *Graph Machine Learning* comes in; they are designed to learn not only from node features but also from the graph's connectivity pattern (graph's structure), enabling models to extract rich representations of the data.

Graph ML unlocks the ability to solve problems that were previously difficult or impossible to solve using traditional methods. For example, predicting which two people in a social network are likely to become friends, classifying types of proteins in a molecular graph, or detecting fraudulent transactions in a financial network; these are all tasks where graph-based methods outperform conventional approaches.

What You Will Learn

The book begins with the fundamentals of graph theory and then delves into the core building blocks of graph machine learning. You will learn how to:

- Construct meaningful graph representations from raw data.
- Different types of tasks that can be solved using graph machine learning.
- Embedding-based graph machine learning technique.
- Learn about the neural network-based graph machine learning technique called Graph Neural Networks (GNNs).
- Explore advanced GNN architectures and techniques for handling real-world challenges like scalability, over-squashing, and noisy data.
- Apply graph machine learning to real applications such as social network analysis and recommendation systems.

Important sections of the book provide simple examples, accompanied by code snippets written using the popular **PyTorch Geometric (PyG)** library. These practical sections are designed to reinforce theoretical concepts and help you implement working models on your own.

Who can benefit from this book?

This book is for a wide range of readers:

- **Working professionals, ML engineers, data scientists, or software engineers** seeking to apply graph machine learning techniques to solve practical problems in industry.
- **Researchers** entering the area of graph machine learning and who are looking for a solid starting point that explains both theory and implementation.
- **Undergraduate/Graduate students** who have completed an introductory machine learning course and want to explore the powerful world of graph-based learning.
- Graph Machine Learning enthusiasts

How to use this book?

This book is designed to be flexible and useful for a wide range of readers, so the way you approach it depends on your background and goals.

If you are new to graphs and graph machine learning but already have a basic understanding of how machine learning algorithms work, we recommend starting from **Chapter 1**. This will introduce you to fundamental concepts about graphs and why learning from graph-structured data is important. If you have already taken a course in graph theory, you may directly start from **Chapter 2**, which dives deeper into graph machine learning concepts without repeating basic graph definitions.

For those who do not have prior knowledge of machine learning itself, we strongly suggest reading **Appendix A: A Brief Recap of Machine Learning** before starting the main chapters. This appendix covers the essential building blocks, such as regression, classification, gradient descent, and neural networks, which form the basis for understanding graph learning.

For **students and researchers** who wish to work deeply in the area of machine learning and explore graph learning as a research topic, the recommended learning path is:

Chapter 1 → Chapter 2 → Chapter 3 → Chapter 4 → Chapter 5 → Chapter 6 → Chapter 7 → Chapter 8.

This path provides a solid foundation starting from graph basics, progressing through GNN fundamentals, advanced architectures, and practical applications, with advanced methods explained in depth.

If you are a **working professional or a researcher from a different field** planning to use graph machine learning as a practical tool for solving problems, we suggest the following reading order:

Chapter 1 → Chapter 2 → Chapter 3 → Chapter 4 → Chapter 5 → Chapter 7 → Chapter 8.

This path covers essential concepts and hands-on implementation without going too deep into theoretical aspects at first. After getting familiar with the basics and practical applications, you can refer to **Chapter 6** later for advanced techniques that help improve performance when needed.

You will also notice certain sections or headings marked with a star (*). These indicate advanced topics that are optional for the scope of this book, and you can safely skip them during a first reading without missing any core concepts.

Throughout the book, you will find **programming assignments** designed to help you implement the concepts practically, regardless of your background. We highly recommend attempting these assignments after each chapter, as they reinforce your understanding and give you hands-on experience before moving to the next topic. **Programming assignments have been provided on online resources and should be downloaded before reading the book.**

In addition, there are **end-of-chapter quizzes** provided to help you check your understanding of key concepts. Some important sections also include **in-chapter quizzes**, especially to help practice and consolidate mathematical ideas.

CHAPTER 1

Introduction to Graph Machine Learning

Key Learning Objectives

- Understand what a graph is and what nodes and edges represent
- Identify important terms associated with graphs, like degree, adjacency, neighborhood, and incidence
- Recognize real-world structures that can be represented as graphs (e.g., social networks, transport systems, neuroscience)
- Understand why traditional machine learning and deep learning models can not be applied to graph-structured data

How can we suggest new friends to a user on Facebook? How do we identify influential users on a social media platform? How do we identify bots on social media? How do we stop the spread of fake news? How can we recommend someone good movies on Netflix? How to use machine learning for drug discovery and predicting molecular properties? How do we identify fraud in a financial network? How to use machine learning to optimize traffic flow? These questions and many more can be effectively answered by modelling our data as Graphs and using Graph

Machine Learning techniques. Let us begin with understanding what graphs are.

1.1 Introduction to Graphs

Graphs are powerful mathematical structures used to model any form of relationship between entities. They can be found in a wide range of real-world applications. For instance, consider the example of a social network (shown in Figure 1.1), where users are represented as entities, and connections between them (friendships or followerships) are relationships. In this example, each user is a node (or vertex), and the connection between two users is an edge. Nodes (users) and Edges (connections) together form a graph. In some literature, graphs are also referred to as networks. Representing data as a graph allows us to effectively understand and analyze important relationships among the nodes of the network. By visualizing the graph, we can uncover patterns like cliques (groups of friends) or influencers (nodes with many connections).

Figure 1.1 **Pictorial representation of a graph**

Source: Copilot

Prompt: A flat, hand drawn vector illustration of a social network graph. Each circle is a node (representing a user), and each line is an edge (representing a connection).

Definition: Graph

A graph $\boldsymbol{G} = (\boldsymbol{V}, \boldsymbol{E})$ consists of a set of nodes V and a set of edges $E \subseteq V \times V$, which represent the relationship between nodes.

Each edge connects two nodes. If the edges have a direction (e.g., a one-way connection like following someone on Twitter), the graph is called a **directed graph**. Otherwise, it is an **undirected graph**. If edges have weights (e.g., the strength of a relationship or distance between nodes), the graph is called a **weighted graph**.

1.1.1 Key terms associated with graphs

- **Degree:** In an undirected graph, the degree of a node is the total number of edges connected to the node. In a directed graph, the in-degree of a node is the number of incoming edges to the node, and the out-degree of a node is the number of outgoing edges from the node. Degree of a node v is denoted by $d(v)$.
- **Incidence:** Incidence refers to the relationship between a node and an edge. A node is said to be incident to an edge if the edge connects that node to another node. Similarly, an edge is said to be incident to a node if the edge is directly connected to the node. For a directed graph, an outgoing edge is called incident from a node, and an incoming edge is called incident to a node.
- **Adjacency:** Two nodes are said to be adjacent if there is an edge connecting them.
- **Neighborhood:** The neighborhood of a node consists of all nodes directly connected to it by an edge. The neighborhood of a node is denoted by $N(v)$.

EXAMPLE

Figure 1.2 is an undirected graph. It has 5 nodes {1, 2, 3, 4, 5} and 5 edges {(1, 2), (2, 3), (1, 4), (2, 4), (3, 5)}; the order in which we write edges of an undirected graph does not matter. Node 2 has degree 3, whereas node 5 has degree 1. What are the degrees of nodes 1, 3, and 4?

Nodes 2 and 3 are incident to the edge (2, 3). Edge (5, 3) is incident to nodes 3 and 5.

Nodes 2 and 3 are adjacent to each other, whereas 5 and 2 are not adjacent to each other.

Neighbourhood of node 4 is given by $N(4) = \{1, 2\}$, and neighbourhood of 2 is given by $N(2) =\{1, 3, 4\}$. What is $N(3)$?

Figure 1.2 **An undirected graph**

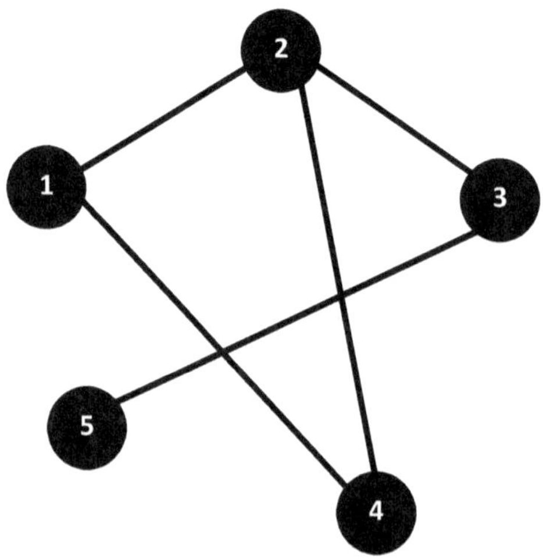

EXAMPLE

Figure 1.3 is a directed graph. It again has 5 nodes, but now it has 6 edges, and the order in which we write the edges does matter. The set of edges for the given graph is {(1, 2), (1, 4), (2, 1), (2, 3), (4, 2), (5, 3)}.

Node 2 has an in-degree of 2 and an out-degree of 2.

Similarly, 3 has an in-degree of 2 and an out-degree of 0.

Edge (4, 2) is incident from 4 and is incident to 2. Nodes 2 and 4 are incident to the edge (4, 2).

Out-neighborhood of node 2 is {3, 1}, and in-neighborhood of 2 is {4, 1}.

Figure 1.3 **A directed graph**

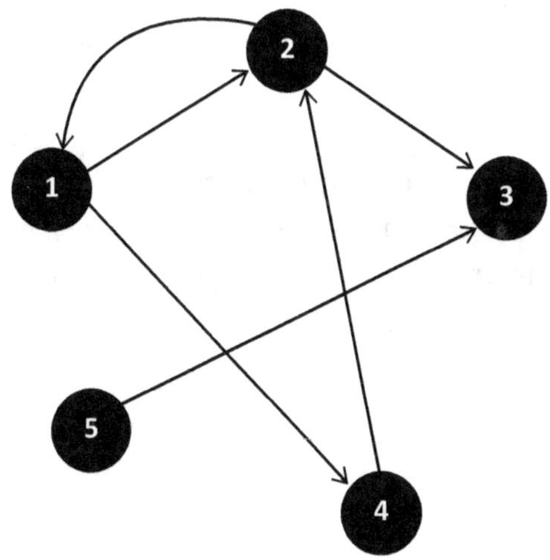

1.2 The Power of Graphs: Real-World Examples of Graphs

In this section, we will look at some important real-world examples that can be modelled as graphs and important questions that can be asked about those graphs:

1.2.1 Social Networks

One of the most natural and intuitive examples of a graph is a social network. As discussed before, in this setting, individuals are represented as nodes, and edges capture the relationships between them. These relationships can be friendships (two users are friends with each other), follows (a user follows another user), or likes (a user liked another user's content). These relationships are crucial because they often tell us more about a person's behavior than their individual attributes. Graphs allow us to ask useful questions like: *Who might become friends in the future? Which groups of people are closely connected?* Understanding such groups can help detect communities, tailor content, or analyze group dynamics. *Who are the most influential individuals in spreading a message?* This can be useful for designing viral marketing strategies or prioritizing information delivery. *Are there any accounts that behave unusually compared to the rest?* Machine learning on graph data can help us answer these important questions about social network data.

1.2.2 Biological Networks

Graphs are also widely used in biology and medicine to represent complex interactions between biological entities. In such networks, nodes can represent genes, proteins, or drugs, while edges capture various types of interactions.

For example, a protein interacting with another protein, or a drug targeting a specific gene. These networks help researchers understand how different components of a biological system work together. Using graphs, one can explore questions like: *Which proteins tend to work closely together?* Helping identify functional groups or pathways. *How might a new drug affect a biological process?* Providing valuable insight into drug discovery or repurposing. Modeling biological systems as graphs brings structure to data that is otherwise too interconnected and complex to interpret easily.

1.2.3 Recommendation System

Graphs can play a powerful role in recommendation systems. In this context, nodes represent users and items such as movies, books, or products, while edges capture the interactions between them, like ratings, clicks, or purchases. This structure helps uncover relationships not just between users and items, but also among users with similar tastes or items with related appeal. For instance, one might ask, *What kind of products is a user likely to enjoy next?* A key question behind most personalized recommendation engines. Even in cases where a user has little history (known as the "cold start" problem), graphs allow us to make educated guesses by examining how similar users interact with the system. Graphs add a relational layer that enhances personalization and discovery.

Figure 1.4 **Modeling the recommendation problem as a graph**

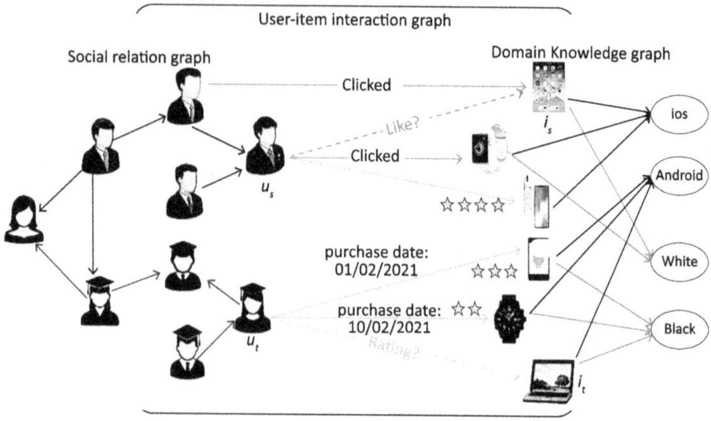

Source: Wang et al., 2021

1.2.4 Transportation and Urban Planning

Transportation systems are naturally suited to graph representation. One may represent intersections, airports, or train stations via nodes of a graph, and edges represent the roads, tracks, or flight paths connecting them. This graph-based view allows planners to ask practical questions like: *What is the shortest or fastest route between two points? Where are the most congested or vulnerable links in the network?* Using graphs helps in optimizing traffic flow, designing efficient public transport routes, and identifying critical infrastructure that needs reinforcement or expansion.

1.2.5 Neuroscience

In neuroscience, graphs are used to model the brain's intricate wiring. Nodes represent individual neurons or larger brain regions, and edges denote synaptic connections or functional relationships between them. These brain graphs help researchers ask questions like: *Which regions of the brain are most central in processing information? How does brain connectivity differ between healthy and diseased states?* Graph-based models are invaluable for mapping the brain, diagnosing neurological conditions, and understanding how different parts of the brain communicate.

1.2.6 Citation and Co-Authorship Network

Graphs are also commonly used to study scientific collaboration and knowledge flow. In a citation network, nodes represent research papers, and edges indicate which paper cites which. In a co-authorship network, nodes are authors, and edges connect researchers who have published together. These graphs allow us to explore questions like: *Which papers have had the most influence in a field? How do research communities form and evolve over time?* Graphs help reveal how ideas spread, which authors serve as connectors between disciplines, and where academic collaboration is thriving.

1.2.7 Financial Network

In the financial world, graphs offer a powerful way to represent and analyze complex networks of transactions. Nodes can represent bank accounts, payment devices, or individual transactions, while edges capture connections between them, such as money transfers or shared identifiers like IP addresses or phone numbers. These graphs help answer critical questions like: *Are there suspicious patterns of transactions among certain accounts?* This can reveal fraudulent rings or coordinated behavior. *Is a particular transaction likely to be risky or unusual?* Enabling early detection of fraud. Graph-based modeling brings structure to scattered financial data and improves the ability to uncover hidden relationships that may indicate financial crime.

1.3 Why Traditional ML Methods Do Not Work Directly for Graphs

Most traditional machine learning models, like decision trees, support vector machines, or even deep neural networks, are built to handle structured data formats such as tables, images, or text. These data types share a few key properties: they have a fixed structure, the size and shape of the input are usually consistent, and each data point is considered independent of the others.

For example, in tabular data, we input one row at a time, say, information about a customer or a product. Each row stands on its own, and the model treats it independently from the rest of the data. This idea that data points can be processed in isolation is known loosely as the independent and identically distributed (i.i.d.) assumption.

Graphs break this assumption. In graphs, the meaning or importance of a data point (like a person in a social network or a protein in a biological system) depends on its connections to others. So instead of feeding in a single data point, we want to feed in a node along with its neighbors, the local structure that gives it context (see Figure 1.5).

One might think we can handle this using deep learning models designed for images or text, since they also consider local neighborhoods. But there's a big difference: in images, each pixel has a well-defined position, and its neighbors are always in fixed places (like above or to the left). In text, words come in a sequence, and the order is important. Graphs, on the other hand, don't follow a fixed structure or order.

Figure 1.5 Contrasting neighborhood structures

Unlike the fixed grid of neighbors for a pixel in an image or the ordered neighbors of a word in a sentence, a node in a graph can have a variable number of unordered neighbors. Red (R), Blue (B), Yellow (Y)

A node can have any number of neighbors, and their arrangement isn't numbered or directional in a predictable way.

These differences create major challenges for applying traditional machine learning algorithms directly to graphs. Algorithms like logistic regression, decision trees, or even neural networks assume that input data points are i.i.d., and that they come in a consistent format, neither of which is true for graph data. Moreover, these models lack the capability to understand or process relational structure; they don't naturally consider how data points are connected to one another.

As a result, applying standard models to graph data without adaptation often leads to poor performance or requires flattening or transforming the graph into a format that loses much of its useful structure. This motivates the need for specialized techniques, like graph-based embeddings and Graph Neural Networks, that can handle the unique properties of graph-structured data more effectively. These specialized techniques will be discussed in the upcoming chapters of the book.

Chapter Summary

- A graph consists of nodes and edges that represent entities and the relationships between them.
- Common graph terms include degree, adjacency, neighborhood, and incidence, which help describe the local structure of nodes.
- Graphs appear in many real-world domains, such as social media, biology, transportation, finance, and more.
- Unlike traditional data formats, graphs have no fixed size or order, and their data points are interdependent, not independent.
- As a result, most traditional ML/DL models (which assume fixed-size, independent input) cannot be applied directly to graphs.
- This motivates the need for graph-specific techniques that respect the relational and irregular nature of graph data.

Quiz

1. **In a graph, what do nodes represent?**
   a. Connections
   b. Entities or objects
   c. Paths
   d. Edges

2. **What term is used for the connection between two nodes in a graph?**
   a. Vertex
   b. Loop
   c. Edge
   d. Degree

3. **In an undirected graph, an edge:**
   a. Has no direction
   b. Has a direction from one node to another
   c. Can only connect self-loops
   d. Is allowed only between nodes of equal degree

4. **In a directed graph, the degree of a node is split into:**
   a. Incident and adjacent degree
   b. Forward and backward degree
   c. In-degree and out-degree
   d. Incoming and outgoing edges (no degrees)

5. **Which of the following is true for a self-loop?**
   a. It connects two different nodes
   b. It connects a node to itself
   c. It is only allowed in weighted graphs
   d. It only appears in trees

6. **The number of edges connected to a node is called its:**
    a. Adjacency
    b. Incidence
    c. Degree
    d. Path length

7. **In an undirected graph, if a node has degree 4, it:**
    a. Is connected to 4 unique neighbors
    b. Has 4 outgoing edges
    c. Can't be a leaf node
    d. Must be part of a cycle

8. **Two nodes are called neighbors if:**
    a. They are in the same cluster
    b. They are directly connected by an edge
    c. They have the same degree
    d. They share a node ID

9. **In a weighted graph, each edge:**
    a. Has a unique ID
    b. Represents only binary connections
    c. Carries a numerical value
    d. Must be bidirectional

10. **Which of the following correctly defines a neighborhood of a node?**
    a. Set of nodes at distance 2
    b. Set of nodes in the same degree class
    c. Set of nodes connected directly to it
    d. Nodes reachable via shortest path

Answers

1 – b	2 – c	3 – a	4 – c	5 – b
6 – c	7 – a	8 – b	9 – c	10 – c

CHAPTER 2

Common Tasks on Graph Data

Key Learning Objectives

- Understand different ways to represent graphs: adjacency matrix, edge list, and feature matrices
- Prepare and structure data for graph-based tasks like node classification and edge prediction
- Apply key evaluation metrics such as accuracy, precision, recall, F1 score, and AUC
- Calculate structural similarity scores such as Common Neighbors, Jaccard Coefficient, and Adamic-Adar Index
- Understand the practical significance of node classification, edge prediction, and the graph classification task

In Chapter 2, we'll explore how to represent graph data in ways that computers can understand and use for machine learning tasks. You'll learn about different formats like adjacency matrices, adjacency lists, and edge lists, as well as their strengths and weaknesses. Once we've covered that, we'll dive into some of the most important tasks you can perform with graph data, like node classification, link prediction, and graph classification. I'll also walk you through how to evaluate the performance of algorithms designed for these tasks. By the end of this chapter, you'll have a firm grasp of how to prepare and analyze graph data for machine learning; this chapter will serve as a foundation for what is to follow in this book.

2.1 Representing Graphs in Data Structures

This section will explore how to represent graphs in forms that computers can efficiently process. These representations are the foundation for implementing machine learning algorithms on graph data.

2.1.1 Adjacency Matrix

The Adjacency matrix is one of the most common methods to represent a graph. An adjacency matrix is a square matrix of the size $|V \times V|$ (number of nodes times the number of nodes). Each row and column corresponds to a node in the graph. The entries in the matrix indicate the presence or absence of an edge between two nodes. For an unweighted graph, 1 at the intersection of the *i-th* row and the *j-th* column means the presence of an edge between nodes i and j. Similarly, 0 means the absence of an edge between i and j. For weighted graphs, the entries can also store the weight of the edge. Let us look at some examples of adjacency matrices.

EXAMPLE 1

Figure 2.1 An undirected graph

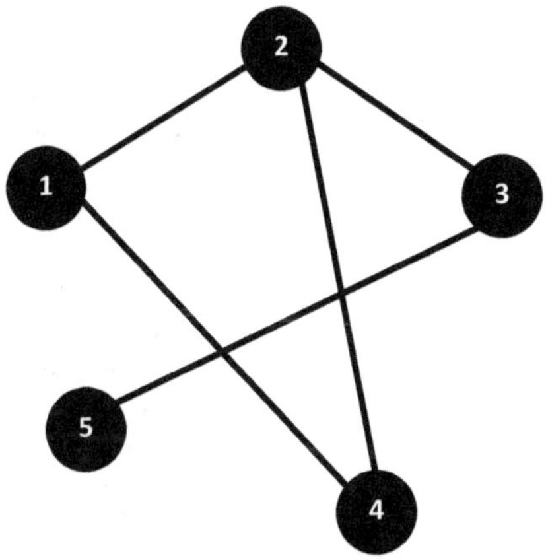

The adjacency matrix for the graph in Figure 2.1 is given by

$$A = \begin{bmatrix} 0 & 1 & 0 & 1 & 0 \\ 1 & 0 & 1 & 1 & 0 \\ 0 & 1 & 0 & 0 & 1 \\ 1 & 1 & 0 & 0 & 0 \\ 0 & 0 & 1 & 0 & 0 \end{bmatrix}$$

$A_{1,2} = 1$ means there is an edge between nodes 1 and 2;
$A_{1,3} = 0$ means there is no connection between nodes 1 and 3.

EXAMPLE 2

Figure 2.2 **A weighted graph**

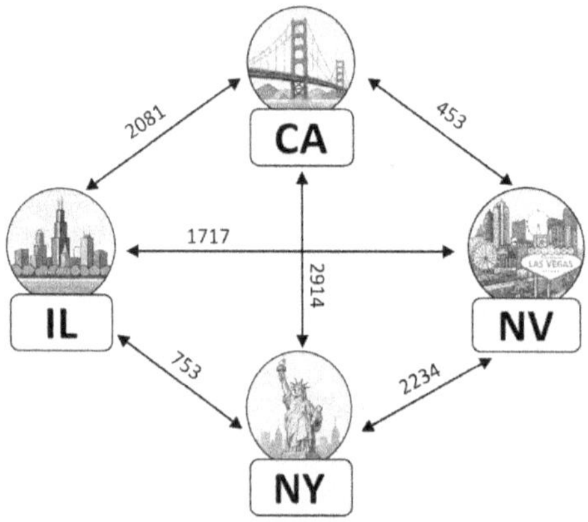

A graph where nodes represent states and edge weight denotes distance in miles.

The adjacency matrix for the graph in Figure 2.2 is given by

$$B = \begin{array}{c} IL \\ CA \\ NV \\ NY \end{array} \begin{bmatrix} 0 & 2081 & 1717 & 753 \\ 2081 & 0 & 453 & 2914 \\ 1717 & 453 & 0 & 234 \\ 753 & 2914 & 234 & 0 \end{bmatrix}$$

$B_{1,2} = 2081$ means the distance between IL and CA is 2081 miles.

The adjacency matrix is simple and intuitive, making it a good choice for dense graphs where most nodes are connected. It allows for constant time complexity when checking for the existence of an edge. However, it is memory-inefficient for sparse graphs, as it requires $O(n^2)$. This inefficiency makes it difficult to scale for large graphs with millions of nodes and edges, limiting its practical use in real-world scenarios.

2.1.2 Edge List

As the name suggests, an edge list is simply a list of all edges of a graph.

> **EXAMPLE**
>
> The edge list for the graph in Figure 2.1 is as follows: {(*1,2*), (*1,4*), (*2,1*), (*2,3*), (*2,4*), (*3,2*), (*3,5*), (*4,1*), (*4,2*), (*5,3*)}.
>
> For an undirected graph, we can simplify this representation by omitting duplicate edges (those in the reverse direction). The edge list can then be written in a more compact form as:
>
> {(*1,2*), (*1,4*), (*2,3*), (*2,4*), (*3,5*)}.
>
> The edge list for the graph in Figure 2.2 is given by:
>
> {(*IL,CA,2081*), (*IL,NV,1717*), (*IL,NY,753*), (*CA,NV,453*), (*CA,NY,2914*), (*NV,NY,2234*)}.

Quiz 2.1

Edge lists are highly effective at storing sparse graphs because of their memory efficiency (because they only store connections between nodes). They are perfect for preliminary research or data sharing because of their simple, adaptable format. Additionally, they can represent both weighted and unweighted graphs by including or omitting a weight column. Edge lists are less effective for dense graphs, though, as adjacency matrices may handle these situations more effectively by avoiding repeated storage of edges. Additionally, they do not have direct node lookup capabilities; instead, one must search the list for neighbors or particular connections, which can be computationally expensive for large graphs. Despite these limitations, edge lists remain a useful option for many graph-related tasks, particularly in tools like NetworkX and PyTorch Geometric, despite these drawbacks.

2.1.3 Feature Matrices and Node/Edge Attributes

When working with real-world graph data, nodes and edges often have additional information associated with them. This information is important for many machine learning tasks, as it helps the model capture and make more informed predictions. For example, in a social network, nodes represent individuals, and their features might include their age, profession, and the number of posts they've made, etc. Similarly, edges can carry attributes related to edge information. For example, in a transportation network, nodes could represent cities, while edges represent roads with attributes such as distance, travel time, or toll costs. These attributes are typically represented using **feature matrices**. A **node feature matrix** consists of one row per node, with each row containing the node's feature values.

On the other hand, an **edge feature matrix** has one row per edge, where each row contains the attributes associated with that edge.

ACTIVITY

Download the online resources for this book and attempt **Programming assignment 2.1**. It covers hands-on implementation of the discussed concepts, including representing graphs and visualizing them using two popular libraries: NetworkX and PyTorch Geometric (PyG). This practical exercise will help solidify your understanding of graph representations and basic operations.

We will now look at some common tasks on graph data that use machine learning algorithms.

2.2 Node Classification

Imagine you're part of a company managing online transactions. An online transaction network is a graph where each node represents a user and edges denote financial transactions between them. Some users in this network may be fraudulent, engaging in activities like money laundering or phishing. Detecting these fraudulent users is crucial for maintaining the integrity of the financial system. Now, the company wants to predict whether a user is fraudulent or legitimate.

In this scenario, the goal is to assign a label to each user (node), for instance, "fraudulent" or "legitimate". However, you don't have this information for every user. What you do have is some labeled data (e.g., a subset of users whose labels you already know based on prior investigations) and access to the transaction graph that connects users.

This is a classic example of a **node classification task**. In this task, the aim is to predict labels for nodes in a graph using both the graph structure and the features of the nodes. It's important to note that in node classification, we work with a single graph, where the relationships between nodes play a crucial role in determining the labels. By leveraging both node features (such as user activity levels or profile data) and the graph structure (connections between users), node classification models can infer patterns that would otherwise remain hidden in traditional tabular data. This makes node classification a powerful tool for many real-world applications, including:

- Identifying communities or interests of users in social networks.
- Categorizing proteins in biological interaction networks.
- Predicting customer churn in business networks.
- Categorizing articles in citation networks based on references and content.

Figure 2.3 **A pictorial representation of the node classification task**

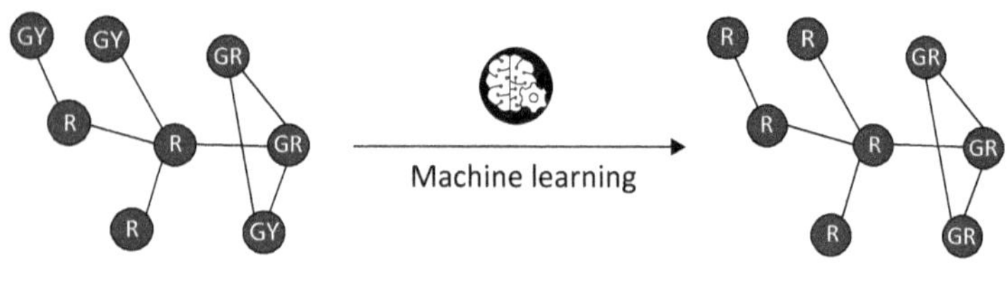

Given labels to some of the nodes [Green (GR) and Red (R) nodes], we want to train a model to predict the labels for the Grey (GY) nodes.

2.2.1 Preparing data for node classification

Once we understand the concept of node classification, the next step is to prepare the data for this task. In real-world scenarios, the graph structure is typically available, but node labels are often only partially observed, with some nodes remaining unlabeled. Our objective is to use the labeled nodes to predict the labels of the unlabeled ones. For example, in Figure 2.3, given a subset of nodes labeled as green or red, our goal is to infer the labels of the grey nodes.

Step-by-step details about data preparation for node classification are as follows:

Understanding the data

Begin by examining the graph data. Identify the nodes, their features, and the available labels. For example, in a social network, nodes might represent users, and features could include profile information, while labels might indicate whether a user belongs to a particular interest group.

Splitting the data

In practice, before deploying our model to the real world, we will use only the labeled nodes to train and evaluate the model's performance. To do so, we divide the labeled nodes into three subsets:

- **Training Set**: This subset contains nodes with known labels, which the model will use to learn.
- **Validation Set**: We mask the label for nodes belonging to this subset; the original masked label is called **ground truth**. We use the trained model to obtain predictions for the validation set (known as predicted labels), compare the predicted labels with the ground truth, and use the result to choose the best hyperparameter.
- **Test Set**: We also mask the labels for this subset. Comparing the ground truth and predicted labels for the test set helps evaluate how well the model performs on unseen data.

Generally, we allocate a larger portion of the data to training. For instance, 60% of the labeled nodes might be used for training, 20% for validation, and 20% for testing.

Feature preparation

It is important to ensure that each node has a feature vector that captures relevant information. If features are missing, they can be created based on the graph's structure (e.g., node degree, aggregated neighborhood information).

Label encoding

Convert the node labels into a format suitable for machine learning algorithms. Categorical labels can be encoded as integers or one-hot vectors. For example, in Figure 2.3, green nodes can be assigned **label 0**, and red nodes can be assigned **label 1**.

Algorithm application

With the data prepared, you can use the training set to fit your chosen algorithm (discussed in upcoming chapters). The validation set helps you tune hyperparameters, and the test set allows you to measure the model's accuracy, precision, recall, or other relevant metrics.

2.2.2 Metrics to evaluate node classification algorithms

In this book, we will explore a variety of node classification algorithms. Figure 2.4 provides a pictorial representation of the node classification pipeline. We use the node classification algorithm to predict labels for the black nodes in a graph that has a few nodes labeled with one of three colors (green, orange, or violet).

Figure 2.4 Pictorial representation of node classification pipeline

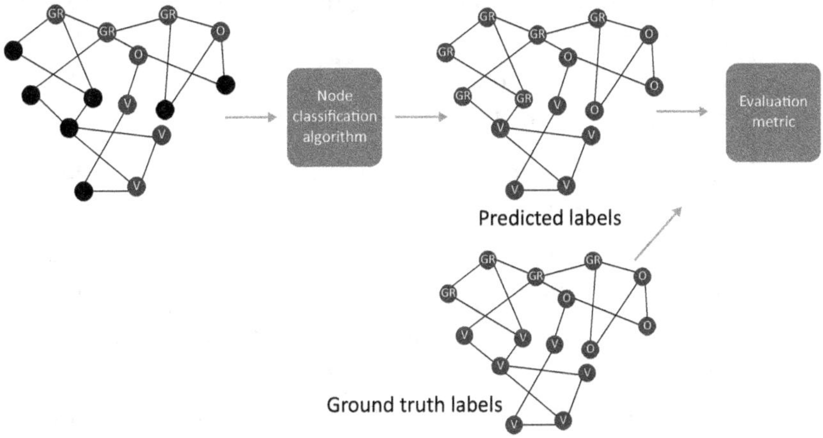

*Green (GR), Orange (O), and Violet (V).

To determine the performance of the algorithm or compare different algorithms, we need a method to evaluate how well they perform. Intuitively, for a good node classification algorithm, the predicted labels should match the ground truth for a large number of test nodes. Let us formalize this intuition and examine some common metrics used to evaluate node classification algorithms.

Accuracy

Accuracy is one of the simplest and most intuitive metrics for evaluating classification tasks. It measures the proportion of correctly classified nodes out of the total number of nodes in the test set.

$$Accuracy = \frac{Number\ of\ Correct\ Predictions}{Total\ Number\ of\ Predictions}$$

EXAMPLE

Consider the graph shown in Figure 2.4. There are 7 test nodes (black-colored nodes), and the algorithm is able to predict 5 test nodes correctly. So, the accuracy of the algorithm in Figure 2.4 is 5/7 = 0.714.

Accuracy is easy to calculate. Consider a graph with 1000 test nodes, out of which 990 nodes have label 0 and 10 nodes have label 1. Now, imagine an algorithm that assigns every node label 0. The accuracy of the algorithm would be 0.99, which is very high. However, the algorithm has failed to correctly classify any nodes of class 1. Although accuracy is widely used, it is not a great evaluation metric for class-imbalanced data.

Confusion Matrix

The Confusion Matrix provides a detailed summary of a number of correct and incorrect predictions. For Figure 2.4, the confusion matrix is structured as a 3x3 table, where rows represent the actual classes (ground truth), and columns represent the predicted classes. Here's a layout for a confusion matrix for Figure 2.4:

	Predicted: Green	Predicted: Orange	Predicted: Violet
Actual: Green	Correctly predicted Green nodes	Green nodes, misclassified as Orange	Green nodes, misclassified as Violet
Actual: Orange	Orange nodes, misclassified as Green	Correctly predicted Orange nodes	Orange nodes, misclassified as Violet
Actual: Violet	Violet nodes, misclassified as Green	Violet nodes, misclassified as Orange	Correctly predicted Violet nodes

EXAMPLE 1

Filling in the exact value according to Figure 2.4 gives:

	Predicted: Green	Predicted: Orange	Predicted: Violet
Actual: Green	1	0	0
Actual: Orange	0	2	0
Actual: Violet	2	0	2

EXAMPLE 2

One can also create a Confusion matrix just for a class; for example, the confusion matrix for class Violet is given by:

	Predicted: Violet	Predicted: Any other color
Actual: Violet	TP (True Positive): Violet was correctly predicted as Violet	FN (False Negative): Violet was misclassified as other colors
Actual: Any other Color	FP (False positive): Other colors misclassified as Violet	TN (True Negative): Other colors correctly predicted as other colors

Filling in exact values according to Figure 2.4 gives:

	Predicted: Violet	Predicted: Any other color
Actual: Violet	TP (True Positive): 2	FN (False Negative): 2
Actual: Any other Color	FP (False positive): 0	TN (True Negative): 3

Precision and Recall

Precision focuses on the quality of the positive predictions. It answers the question: Of all the nodes predicted to belong to a specific class, how many actually do? For a given class, Precision is calculated as:

$$\text{Precision (for a class)} = \frac{TP}{TP+FP}$$

Recall, on the other hand, measures the algorithm's ability to correctly identify all nodes belonging to a specific class. It answers the question: Of all the nodes that truly belong to a specific class, how many did the model correctly predict? For a given class, Recall is calculated as:

$$\text{Recall (for a class)} = \frac{TP}{TP+FN}$$

EXAMPLE

For the Violet class, Precision = $\frac{2}{2+0}$ = 1, and Recall = $\frac{2}{2+2}$ = 0.5. A similar calculation for the Green class shows that precision = 0.33 and recall = 1.

F1-Score

Precision and Recall are essential metrics, but they offer different perspectives. However, in many scenarios, we need a single metric that balances both. This is where the **F1 Score** comes in. The **F1 Score** is the harmonic mean of Precision and Recall, giving equal weight to both. It is defined as:

$$F1-Score(for\, a\, class) = 2 \times \frac{Precision \times Recall}{Precision + Recall}$$

The harmonic mean ensures that the F1 Score is high only when both Precision and Recall are high.

EXAMPLE

F1-score for the Violet class is given by

$2 \times \frac{1 \times 0.5}{1 + 0.5} = 2 \times \frac{0.5}{1.5} \approx 0.667$, similarly for the green class, the F1-score is 0.5, and for the Orange class, it is 1.

Macro and Micro F1 score

Quiz 2.2

In multi-class classification tasks, such as our example with three classes (green, orange, violet), evaluating the overall performance of the model requires aggregating the F1 Scores across all classes. Two common approaches for this aggregation are the Macro F1 Score and the Micro F1 Score.

The **Macro F1 Score** is the unweighted average of the F1 Scores for all classes. It treats each class equally, regardless of the number of samples in each class.

$$Macro\ F1 = \frac{1}{Number\ of\ classes} \times (Sum\ of\ F1 - score\ for\ all\ classes)$$

EXAMPLE

The macro F1-score for the graph in Figure 2.4 is given by $\frac{1}{3} \times (0.667 + 0.5 + 1) = \frac{2.167}{3} = 0.722.$

The **Micro F1 Score**, on the other hand, calculates a single F1 Score for the entire dataset by considering all true positives, false positives, and false negatives across all classes. This approach is weighted by the size of each class, giving more importance to classes with more samples.

EXAMPLE

For the graph in Figure 2.4, the Total TP, FP, and FN are given by

Label	TP (True positive)	FP (False positive)	FN (False negative)
Green	1	2	0
Orange	2	0	0
Violet	2	0	2
Total	5	2	2

So, total precision is $\frac{Total\ Tp}{Total\ Tp + Total\ FP} = \frac{5}{5+2} = \frac{5}{7}$; and the total recall is given by $\frac{Total\ \ Tp}{Total\ \ Tp + Total\ \ FN} = \frac{5}{5+2} = \frac{5}{7}$.

The Micro F1 score is defined as

$$Micro\ F1 = 2 \times \frac{Total\ precision \times Total\ recall}{Total\ precision + Total\ recall}$$

For our example, the Micro f1 score is $2 \times \frac{\frac{5}{7} \times \frac{5}{7}}{2 \times \frac{5}{7}} = \frac{5}{7}$

The Macro and Micro F1 Scores offer complementary insights into model performance. Macro F1 is useful for understanding performance balance across classes, while Micro F1 emphasizes overall performance weighted by class size. In practice, both are often reported to give a holistic view of the model's strengths and weaknesses. For now, you have learned how to evaluate the performance of node classification techniques that will be discussed in the upcoming chapters.

2.3 Edge Prediction

Have you ever noticed how Facebook suggests "People You May Know"? These suggestions often feel spot-on, like an old classmate or someone who works at the same company.

But how does Facebook figure this out? The answer lies in a concept called **edge prediction** in graph learning (Edge prediction is also referred to as **link prediction**). Imagine that Facebook represents its users as a graph. Each user is a node (a point in the graph). A friendship between two users is represented as an edge (a line connecting two nodes).

If you're not already friends with someone, there is no edge between your node and theirs. Edge prediction is the task of predicting whether such a connection (an edge) should exist. Essentially, it tries to figure out if two nodes (people, in this case) are likely to form a connection in the future. Edge prediction has many practical applications. Beyond recommending friends on social networks, here are a few examples:

- Recommender Systems: Suggesting items to users, such as movies on Netflix or products on Amazon, by predicting relationships between users and items.
- Fraud Detection: Identifying suspicious transactions in financial networks by spotting unusual or unlikely connections between entities.
- Biological Research: Predicting interactions between proteins or genes in biological networks to help in drug discovery and understanding diseases.

Figure 2.5 Example of a link prediction task

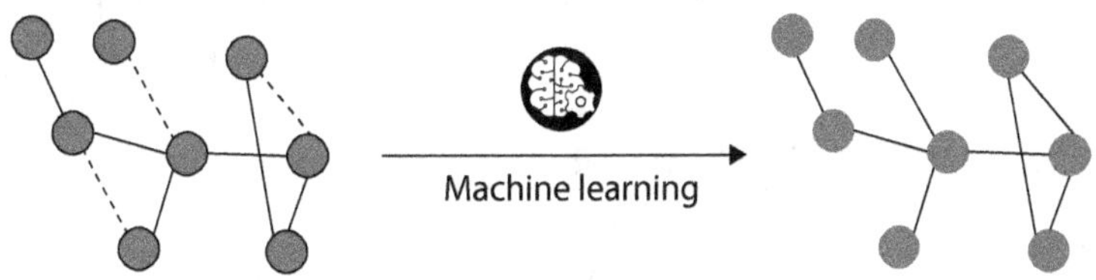

Dotted lines are not present in the graph initially, and we want to predict which of these dotted lines will actually become an edge in the future. We intend to train a model to get the desired graph.

2.3.1 Preparing data for edge prediction

In edge prediction, the goal is to predict missing or potential edges in a graph based on its structure and features. Since we only have access to the graph's structure at a single point in time, we simulate missing edges to test whether an algorithm can recover them effectively. Step-by-step details about preparing data for edge prediction are as follows:

Simulating missing edges

To evaluate an edge prediction algorithm, we begin by "hiding" some edges in the graph. These edges are removed and treated as the test set. A portion of existing edges (e.g., 10-20%) is randomly selected and removed. These removed edges form the **positive examples** in the test set. However, just predicting existing edges isn't sufficient. To ensure a meaningful evaluation, we also create **negative examples** by randomly sampling pairs of nodes that are not connected in the graph. These negative examples represent non-existent edges.

Scoring and ranking

Once the positive and negative examples of edges are prepared, the algorithm assigns a **score** to each potential edge (both positive and negative examples). The score indicates the likelihood of an edge existing between two nodes. Structural Similarity-based scoring is covered in Section 2.3.2.

Selecting edges for prediction

To determine which edges are predicted as existing, a **threshold** is applied to the ranked list. Edges with scores above the threshold are classified as predicted edges.

Alternatively, the top-k edges (where k is the number of positive edges in the test set) are selected as predictions.

2.3.2 Scoring and ranking: Structural similarity measures

In this section, we will elaborate on "Scoring and Ranking." Scoring and ranking algorithms can be divided into two classes: 1. Machine learning-based methods, which will be discussed in upcoming chapters; and 2. Structural similarity measures, which are simple but useful in predicting edges in a graph. These methods rely solely on the graph's structure to compute the likelihood of an edge existing between two nodes. Some of the commonly used structural similarity measures are:

Common Neighbors

As the name suggests, the common neighbor score between two nodes is the number of common neighbors between these two nodes. The score is mathematically calculated as

$$S_{CN}(u,v) = |N(u) \cap N(v)|$$

where $N(u)$ and $N(v)$ represent the set of neighbors of nodes u and v, respectively. The idea behind common neighbors is intuitive: two nodes are more likely to form an edge if they share many neighbors.

A use case of such a score is in social networks; if two people have many mutual friends, they are more likely to connect.

EXAMPLE

For the graph in Figure 2.6,

$S_{CN}(1,3) = |N(1) \cap N(3)| = |\{2,4\} \cap \{2,5\}| = |\{2\}| = 1$; $\boldsymbol{S}_{CN}(1,5) = |\phi| = 0$. Similarly

$S_{CN}(2,5)=1$, $S_{CN}(3,4)=1$, $S_{CN}(4,5)=0$. (1,3) and (2,5) have higher scores than other nonexistent edges; hence, as per common neighbor scores, (1,3) and (2,5) will form edges in the future.

Figure 2.6 An undirected graph

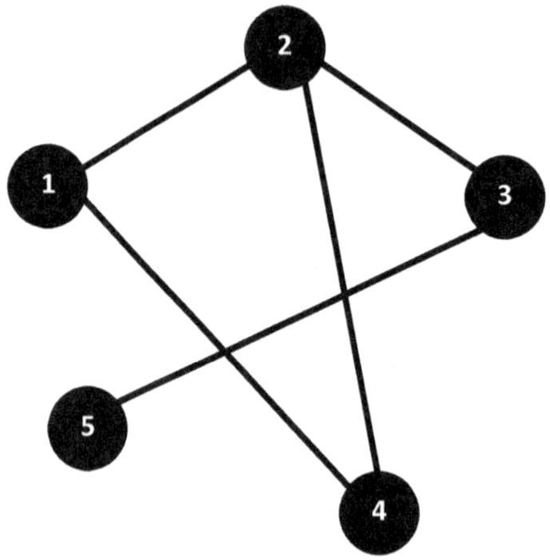

Jaccard Coefficient

Consider an example where Alice and Bob, living in different cities, have a habit of making many friends on a social networking site. Both of them have more than 10,000 friends, with only 4 friends in common. Now, consider another scenario where Allison and Tara study at the same college and have a much smaller circle of friends; in fact, both have fewer than 10 friends, of whom 3 are common. It's intuitive that Allison and Tara are more likely to become friends compared to Alice and Bob. This is because Allison and Tara share 3 common friends out of a total of fewer than 10, whereas Alice and Bob have only 4 common friends out of more than 10,000. If we used the common neighbor count as a measure of potential friendship, it would misleadingly suggest that Alice and Bob have a stronger connection simply because they have more common friends in absolute terms. However, the Jaccard coefficient provides a better perspective. It not only considers the number of common friends but also accounts for the total number of friends both individuals have. The **Jaccard coefficient** measures the similarity between two nodes by dividing the number of common neighbors (between two nodes) by the total number of unique neighbors (between two nodes). It is mathematically given by:

$$S_{JC}(u,v) = \frac{|N(u) \cap N(v)|}{|N(u) \cup N(v)|}$$

This metric normalizes the common neighbor's score, making it useful for comparing nodes with varying degrees. A use case of such a score is in a recommendation system; this measure might identify two users with overlapping interests based on the items they have interacted with.

EXAMPLE

For the graph in Figure 2.6,

$S_{JC}(1,3) = \frac{|N(1) \cap N(3)|}{|N(1) \cup N(3)|} \frac{|\{2,4\} \cap \{2,5\}|}{|\{2,4\} \cup \{2,5\}|} = \frac{|\{2\}|}{|\{2,4,5\}|} = \frac{1}{3}$;

$S_{JC}(1,5) = |\phi| = 0$. Similarly $S_{JC}(2,5) = \frac{1}{3}$, $S_{JC}(3,4) = \frac{1}{3}$,

$S_{CN}(4,5) = 0$.

As per the Jaccard coefficient, (1,5), (2,5), and (1,3) have equal chances of becoming friends in the future.

Preferential Attachment

Preferential attachment is based on the idea that high-degree nodes are more likely to form new edges. The preferential attachment score for two nodes is a product of the size of the neighborhood sets of the two nodes. The score is mathematically computed as:

$$S_{PA}(u,v) = |N(u)| \times |N(v)|$$

A use case of such a score is in citation networks; well-known papers with many citations are more likely to be cited by new papers.

> **EXAMPLE**
>
> For the graph in Figure 2.6, $S_{PA}(1,3)=|\{2,4\}|\times|\{2,5\}|=2\times2=4$; $S_{PA}(1,5)=2\times1=2$. Similarly $S_{PA}(2,5)=3$, $S_{PA}(3,4)=4$, $S_{PA}(4,5)=2$. As per preferential attachment scores, (1,3) and (3,4) are more likely to be future edges than others.

Adamic-Adar Index

Recall the example we discussed while defining the Jaccard coefficient; we said Allison and Tara have 3 common friends. What if their common friends include Alice and Bob? Common nodes have many connections and are often not useful. So, Adamic-Adar proposes penalizing common neighbors with a high degree. The Adamic-Adar index assigns higher importance to common neighbors that have fewer connections. It is calculated as:

$$S_{AA}(u,v) = \sum_{W \in N(u) \cap N(v)} \frac{1}{\log(|N(w)|)}$$

Here, w represents a common neighbor. log (|N(w)|) is the degree of the node w.

EXAMPLE

For the graph in Figure 2.6,

$$S_{AA}(1,3) = \sum_{w \in \{2\}} \frac{1}{log(|N(w)|)} = \frac{1}{log(3)}; S_{CN}(1,5) = 0.$$

Similarly

$$S_{CN}(2,5) = \frac{1}{log(2)}, S_{CN}(3,4) = \frac{1}{log(3)}, S_{CN}(4,5) = 0.$$

As per the Adamic-Adar score, there should be a potential edge between nodes 3 and 4.

Katz Score*

The Katz score considers all paths between two nodes, assigning shorter paths with higher weights. It is defined as:

$$S_{KA}(u,v) = \sum_{l=1}^{\infty} \beta^{l} |Paths_{l}(u,v)|$$

where $Paths_{l}(u,v)$ is the set of all paths of length l between u and v, and β is a decay factor that controls the contribution of longer paths.

One can use any of these scores based on their application and needs. For more information on structural similarity measures, please refer to Liben-Nowell D. & Kleinberg J. (2003).

2.3.3 Evaluation metrics for edge prediction algorithms

After we have obtained scores for every edge, either using a structural similarity measure or via a learning algorithm, the next step is to evaluate how accurate these scores are. Recall that in the test set, we have positive edges (actual edges in the graph) and negative edges (non-existent edges). What we want is for the score of positive edges to be more than that of negative edges.

AUC

AUC is one of the most widely used metrics for edge prediction. It measures the ability of the algorithm to distinguish between positive edges (PE) and negative edges (NE). To calculate AUC, we look at every pair of positive edges and negative edges, and we assign points as follows: 1 point if score(pe)>score(ne); -1 if score(pe)<score(ne); 0.5 if score(pe)=score(ne). AUC is the average of these points over all pairs of positive and negative edges.

$$AUC = \frac{\sum_{pe,ne} 1[S(pe) > S(ne)] - \sum_{pe,ne} 0 * [S(pe) < S(ne)] + 0.5 \times \sum_{pe,ne} 1[S(pe) = S(ne)]}{\# pe \times \# ne}$$

EXAMPLE

For a graph having 5 nodes, we have the following test set:
Positive edges: {(1,2),(2,3),(4,5)}
Negative edges: {(1,4),(2,5),(3,4)}

And let the predicted scores by some algorithm be:
(1,2):0.9,(2,3):0.3,(4,5):0.7 (positive)
(1,4):0.8,(2,5):0.4,(3,4):0.2 (negative)

Now, let's compare the predicted score for every pair of positive and negative edges and assign them points:

S(1,2)>S(1,4): 1 point; S(1,2)>S(2,5): 1 point;
S(1,2)>S(3,4): 1 point;
S(2,3)<S(1,4): 0 point; S(2,3)<S(2,5): 0 point;
S(2,3)>S(3,4): 1 point;
S(4,5)<S(1,4): 0 point; S(4,5)>S(2,5): 1 point;
S(4,5)>S(3,4): 1 point;

Quiz 2.3

By definition,

$$AUC = \frac{\text{sum of all points}}{\text{Total number of edge non edge pair}} = \frac{3+1=2}{9} = \frac{6}{9} \approx 0.667$$

For most practical graphs, the number of negative edges is much larger than the number of positive edges. In such a scenario, we see that AUC is very forgiving. For example, consider a test set with 10 positive edges and 100 negative edges; a prediction algorithm scores them in such a way that the top 10 scores are negative edges, followed by 10 positive edges, and then followed by the remaining 90 negative edges. AUC here is $\frac{90*10-0*10}{10*100}=0.9$, which is high, even though no positive edge was included in the top 10.

Precision at k (Pr@k)

Precision at *k* measures how many of the top *k* predicted edges are actual edges. This metric is especially useful when only the top recommendations are of interest.

$$Pr@k = \frac{\#\ positive\ edges\ in\ top\ k}{k}$$

To calculate Pr@k, the first step is to rank scores in descending order and then count the number of positive edges in the top k.

EXAMPLE

Using the same graph and prediction scores as in the previous example for AUC, the ranked list of scores can be written as follows: (1,2):pe>(1,4):ne>(4,5):pe>(2,5):ne>(2,3):pe>(3,4):ne

$$Pr@2 = \frac{\#\ positive\ edges\ in\ top\ 2}{2} = \frac{1}{2} = 0.5$$

Similarly

$$Pr@3 = \frac{2}{3}; Pr@4 = \frac{1}{2}; Pr@5 = \frac{3}{5}; Pr@6 = \frac{1}{2}$$

Average Precision

Average precision is an extension of precision that considers the ranking of all predicted edges. It computes the average precision across all positive edges and provides a single score. The average is calculated only at positions that contain positive edges and not at all positions.

$$Average\,Precision = \frac{\sum_{\{k:pe\ is\ at\ k\}} Pr@k}{\#pe}$$

Average precision is a harsher measure than AUC and is more sensitive to perturbations in ranking.

EXAMPLE

Using the same graph and prediction scores as presented in the AUC example,

$$Average\ precision = \frac{Pr@1 + Pr@3 + Pr@5}{3} = \frac{1 + \frac{2}{3} + \frac{3}{5}}{3} = \frac{2.2667}{3} = 0.756$$

See that we add precision only at positions where we have positive edges.

ACTIVITY

Download the online resources for this book and attempt **Programming Assignment 2.2.** It will help you reinforce the concepts learned in this section (related to edge prediction) and practically apply them in your work.

2.4 Graph Classification

Imagine you're working for a pharmaceutical company, and your task is to determine whether a new molecule could be a potential drug. Molecules can be represented as graphs, where atoms are nodes and bonds are edges. To classify whether a molecule has the desired properties, you need to look at the entire structure of the graph, not just individual nodes or edges. This is where graph classification comes into play.

Graph classification is the task of assigning a single label to an entire graph. Unlike node or edge prediction, where we focus on parts of a graph, here, the goal is to analyze the graph as a whole. This problem arises in many real-world scenarios, such as:

- **Molecule Property Prediction:** Classifying whether a molecule has therapeutic potential, toxicity, or other chemical properties.
- **Social Network Analysis:** Identifying types of social networks, such as distinguishing between professional and personal networks.
- **Document Categorization:** Representing text documents as graphs (e.g., words as nodes and co-occurrences as edges) and classifying them into categories like sports, politics, or entertainment.

Graph classification typically involves extracting patterns or features from the graph structure, such as connectivity, node properties, and subgraph motifs. These features help models understand the graph's overall characteristics, enabling accurate predictions.

Graph classification does not require an extra step in data preparation and uses the same evaluation metric as node classification. Further details will be discussed in Chapter 5.

2.5 Unsupervised Graph Tasks

While tasks like node classification and edge prediction rely on ground truth labels for training, many real-world scenarios involve networks with absolutely no labeled data. In these situations, unsupervised learning techniques are essential to uncover hidden structures, patterns, and intrinsic properties of the graph. Two of the most prominent unsupervised tasks in this domain are Community Detection and Graph Anomaly Detection.

Community Detection (Graph Clustering): In many networks, nodes naturally tend to form tightly knit groups. Community detection is the process of identifying these clusters, where nodes within a group are densely connected to one another but sparsely connected to nodes outside the group.

- **Objective:** Partition the graph into distinct subgraphs that maximize internal edge density and minimize cross-community connections.
- **Real World Applications:** Identifying distinct social circles within a larger social network, isolating functional modules in protein interaction networks, or segmenting customers based on shared purchasing behavior.

Graph Anomaly Detection: Graphs are highly effective at modeling normal operational behaviors and structural regularities. Consequently, structural deviations from these norms often indicate anomalies. Graph anomaly detection aims to identify nodes, edges, or subgraphs that behave significantly differently from the majority of the network.

- **Objective:** Score and flag structural outliers without relying on historical labeled examples of those anomalies.
- **Real World Applications:** Spotting fraud rings in financial transaction networks, detecting coordinated bot attacks in cybersecurity, or identifying malfunctioning sensors in a localized infrastructure grid.

These unsupervised techniques provide powerful, standalone tools for extracting preliminary insights and understanding the fundamental topology of raw graph data.

Chapter Summary

- Graphs can be represented using adjacency matrices, edge lists, or feature matrices.
- Node classification involves predicting labels for nodes using both structure and node features.
- Data preparation includes train/validation/test split, label encoding, and feature engineering.
- Evaluation metrics for node classification include accuracy, confusion matrix, precision, recall, F1 score, macro-F1, and micro-F1.
- Edge prediction identifies potential or missing links in a graph and is evaluated using AUC, Precision@k, and Average Precision.
- Structural similarity measures such as Common Neighbors, Jaccard Coefficient, Preferential Attachment, Adamic-Adar Index, and Katz Score are simple yet effective tools for edge prediction.
- Graph classification assigns a single label to an entire graph and is useful in applications like molecule property prediction and social network analysis.

Quiz

1. Write down the adjacency matrix and edge list for the following graphs:

   a.

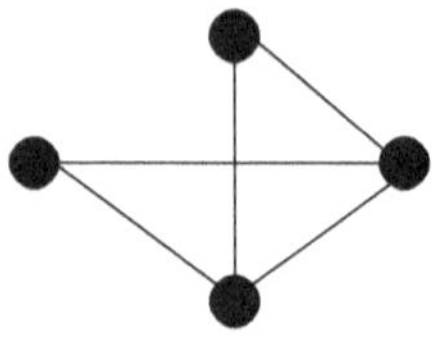

   b.

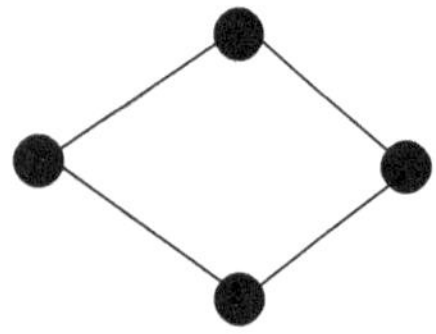

2. In a movie recommendation graph, the nodes represent users, and the edges represent relationships between users based on shared preferences or interactions. For example, an edge might exist between two users if they have rated similar movies or if they have interacted with each other within the platform.

   We aim to classify users into two classes based on their preferred movie genres. The two classes are Class 0: Fans of Action Movies, and Class 1: Fans of Comedy Movies.

   A node classification algorithm was applied, and the confusion matrix summarizing the results is given below:

	Predicted Class 0	Predicted Class 1
True Class 0	50	10
True Class 1	15	25

   Calculate the following:

   a. Overall accuracy of the model

   b. Precision and recall for each class

   c. F1-score of each class

   d. Total precision and recall

   e. Macro F1 and Micro F1 score

3. **Imagine you are working on a fraud detection system for a financial network. Each node in the network represents a user, and the goal is to classify users into one of four categories based on their activity patterns: Genuine Users (Class 1), Low-Risk Fraudsters (Class 2), High-Risk Fraudsters (Class 3), and Unknown Activity (Class 4).**

   You train a node classification algorithm and evaluate its performance on a test dataset. The confusion matrix summarizing the results is provided below:

Predicted	Class 1	Class 2	Class 3	Class 4
Actual Class 1	50	5	2	3
Actual Class 2	10	40	5	5
Actual Class 3	2	3	30	10
Actual Class 4	1	4	8	50

   Calculate the following:

   a. Overall accuracy of the model
   b. Precision and recall for each class
   c. F1-score of each class
   d. Total precision, total recall, Micro F1, and Macro F1 score

Solutions:

Question 1 Answer

1. The solution to this question is not unique and will change depending on the numbering assigned to the nodes. One of the solutions is given by:

   a) The adjacency matrix is given by the matrix A (or its permutations)

$$A = \begin{bmatrix} 0 & 1 & 1 & 0 \\ 1 & 0 & 1 & 1 \\ 1 & 1 & 0 & 1 \\ 0 & 1 & 1 & 0 \end{bmatrix}$$

Edge list is given by {(1,2), (1,3), (2,1), (2,3), (2,4), (3,1), (3,2), (3,4), (4,2), (4,3)}

b) Adjacency matrix A is given by

$$A = \begin{bmatrix} 0 & 1 & 0 & 1 \\ 1 & 0 & 1 & 0 \\ 0 & 1 & 0 & 1 \\ 1 & 0 & 1 & 0 \end{bmatrix}$$

Edge list is given by {(1,2), (1,4), (2,1), (2,3), (3,2), (3,4), (4,3), (4,1)}

Question 2 Answers

A. **Overall accuracy of the model:** 0.75

B. **Precision and recall for each class:** For class 0: Precision = 0.769, Recall = 0.833, For class 1: Precision = 0.714, Recall = 0.625

C. **F1-score of each class:** Class = 0.799, Class 1 = 0.666

D. **Total precision** = 0.75 & Total recall = $\frac{75}{75+25} = 0.75$

E. **Macro F1 score** ≈ 0.733 & Micro F1 score = 0.75

Question 3 Answer

A. **Overall accuracy of the model:** 0.7456

B. **Precision and recall for each class:**

Class 1: Precision ≈ 0.79, Recall ≈ 0.83

Class 2: Precision ≈ 0.77, Recall ≈ 0.67

Class 3: Precision = 0.67, Recall = 0.67

Class 4: Precision ≈ 0.74, Recall ≈ 0.79

C. **F1-score of each class:**

Class 1: 0.81

Class 2: 0.71

Class 3: 0.67

Class 4: 0.76

D. **Total precision, total recall, Micro F1, and Macro F1 score:** 0.7456, Micro F1 ≈ 0.746, Macro F1 ≈ 0.740

CHAPTER 3

Node Embedding Techniques

Key Learning Objectives

- Understanding the challenges of applying traditional machine learning (ML) to graph data
- Exploring the motivation and methodology behind graph embeddings
- Learning foundational embedding techniques, including Graph Factorization and GraRep
- Understanding random walk–based embedding approaches such as DeepWalk and Node2Vec
- Examining how edge embeddings can be derived from node embeddings
- Gaining practical insight into designing similarity and closeness measures

Graph-structured data often carries rich information through both node features and the underlying structure of connections. However, applying classical machine learning algorithms directly to such data is non-trivial due to assumptions like fixed input size and independent data points. This chapter focuses on techniques that help convert graph data into a format suitable for traditional machine learning: **node embeddings**. The central idea is to learn vector representations for graph nodes that preserve structural or functional similarity.

By now, we are convinced that graphs are an important data structure—many real-world problems naturally take the form of graphs, and even problems that are not inherently graphs can often be modeled as one. However, applying classical machine learning (ML) algorithms (such as logistic regression, SVMs, or multilayer perceptrons) directly to graph data is often difficult, or even impossible, for the following reasons:

- **ML algorithms assume independent and identically distributed (i.i.d.) data points, while graph nodes are inherently dependent on each other.**

  The very structure of a graph encodes relationships between nodes through edges. In some cases, these relationships alone can provide meaningful information even if no external node features are available. For example, in Figure 3.1, even without node-specific attributes, we can reasonably infer that nodes 1 and 2 should have the same label (red) and node 3 should have a different label (green), purely based on graph connectivity. Traditional ML models, which assume independence, fail to leverage this structural information.
- **Graphs do not have a fixed shape or size.**
  Unlike structured data like images or tabular datasets, where the input dimensions are well-defined, graphs can grow, shrink, or have varying structures. If we attempt to apply deep learning techniques, such as fully connected neural networks, we immediately run into the issue of defining a fixed-size input layer—something that is not straightforward for graphs.

- **Graphs are permutation invariant, but traditional ML algorithms are not.**
  A graph's adjacency matrix is a common way to represent its structure, but it depends on the order in which nodes are indexed. If we permute the adjacency matrix by reordering nodes, we obtain a different matrix representation for the same graph. However, standard machine learning models do not handle such permutations naturally. For example, if we construct a feature vector for a node where each entry represents the degree of a neighboring node, swapping two neighbors in the vector should not change the meaning of the input, but classical ML models would treat it as a different input.

Given these challenges, there are two main approaches to applying machine learning on graphs:

1. Design specialized ML algorithms that inherently work with graph structures, addressing the three challenges mentioned above. This is the foundation of Graph Neural Networks (GNNs), which we will explore in later chapters.
2. Transform graphs into a representation suitable for traditional machine learning models. This approach allows us to leverage the rich set of existing ML algorithms and techniques. One intuitive way to achieve this is to represent each node as a vector in R^d. These vector representations—known as node embeddings—can then be fed into standard ML models for tasks like classification, graph classification, and edge prediction. We will explore these embedding techniques in the current chapter.

Figure 3.1 **A graph where nodes do not have features**

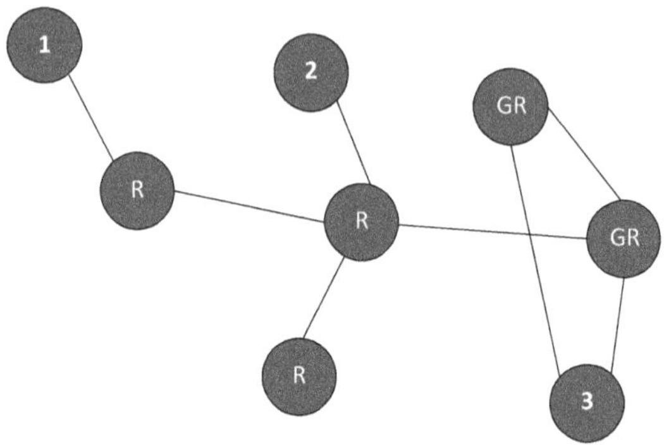

Just by looking at the graph, one may infer that nodes 1 and 2 should be labeled red (R), whereas 3 must be labeled green (GR). Traditional ML models can not make such predictions based on important structural information.

3.1 Node Embedding Techniques

Let *G=(V,E)* be a graph where *V* denotes the set of nodes and *E* denotes the set of edges. One way to tackle the challenge of applying machine learning to graph data is to map every node to a vector in $R^d(d<<|V|)$, where this vector representation of a node is called its embedding. Standard/ Traditional Machine learning algorithms can then operate in this embedded space. This mapping should ensure that "similar" nodes in the graph are positioned "close" to each other in the embedding space. The definition of similarity between nodes and closeness in the embedding space varies across different node embedding techniques. In general, the goal is to ensure that nodes that are structurally or functionally similar in the graph are mapped close together in the embedding space.

Transforming a graph into an embedding space

To represent a graph in an embedding space, we need to define four key components:

1. **Embedding function (Encoder function)**
   We need a function *EMB:* $V \rightarrow R^d$ that maps every node in the graph to a vector in R^d. This function, called the embedding function, is what we aim to learn. The embedding of a node v_i is denoted by z_i.
2. **Similarity measure in the original graph**
   To ensure that nodes mapped close together in the embedding space are actually similar in the original graph, we need a way to define the similarity between nodes in the graph. This is done using a function $S_G: V \times V \rightarrow R^+$, which assigns a similarity score to each node pair.
3. **Closeness measure in the embedding space (Decoder function)**
   Once nodes are mapped to vectors, we need a way to measure how close or similar two vectors are in the embedding space. This is handled by the **decoder function**, represented as $C: R^d \times R^d \rightarrow R^+$. This function computes a similarity score between two node embeddings.

Figure 3.2 Illustration for graph embedding

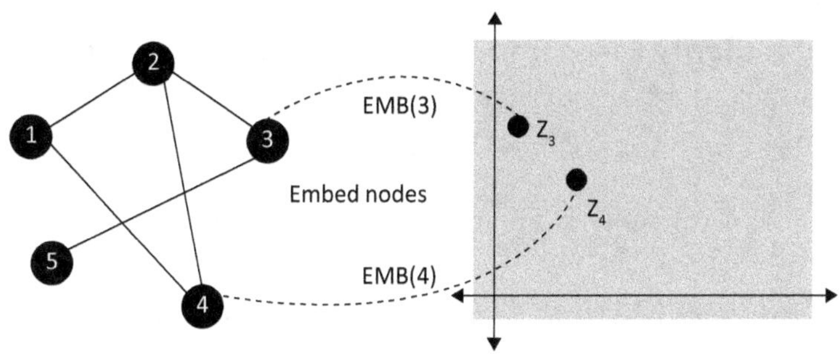

The goal is to learn an embedding function that preserves similarity.

4. **Loss function (Reconstruction error)**

   To ensure that our embeddings preserve the relationships in the original graph, we define a **loss function** $l: R^{+}\times R^{+} \longrightarrow R^{+}$. The loss function compares the similarity score computed in the embedding space $C(z_i,z_j)$ with the original similarity score $S_G(v_i,v_j)$ from the graph. The goal is to **train** the embedding function so that the similarity scores in the embedding space match the similarity scores in the graph. Mathematically, we want:

$$C\left(EMB(v_i), EMB(v_j)\right) = C(z_i,z_j) \approx S_G(v_i,v_j)$$

To achieve this, we minimize the total loss over a set of training node pairs D:

$$L = \sum_{(v_{i,}v_j)\in D} l\left(C(z_{i,}z_j), S_G(v_{i,}v_j)\right)$$

Most approaches minimize the loss using stochastic gradient descent; some methods can also be effectively optimized using more specialized methods (like matrix factorization). This process ensures that the learned embeddings capture meaningful patterns from the graph structure. Let's look at some examples of embedding techniques.

Graph Factorization (GF) [Ahmed et al., 2013]

The **Similarity Measure** $S_G(v_i,v_j)$ for Graph factorization is the adjacency matrix entry:

$$S_G(v_i,v_j) = A_{ij}$$

recall $A_{ij} = 1$ if there is an edge between v_i and v_j, otherwise $A_{ij} = 0$.

Closeness Measure $C(z_i,z_j)$ for Graph factorization is measured using the dot product of their embeddings:

$$C(z_i,z_j) = z_i^{T} z_j$$

Loss Function $l(C,S_G)$ for Graph factorization is the square of the difference between the similarity measure and closeness measure.

$$l = \sum_{(v_i, v_j) \in D} (A_{ij} - z_i^T z_j)^2$$

Embedding can now be obtained by optimizing the loss function by either stochastic gradient descent or using Singular value decomposition (SVD) approximation [SVD is a classical topic in Linear Algebra, for a simple and comprehensive explanation of SVD, please refer to the book Linear Algebra by Friedberg et. al. One may also refer to a lecture by Prof. Gilbert Strang on the topic (course 18.06 freely available on YouTube).

GraRep [Cao et. al., 2015]

In graphs, the neighbors of a node v are also referred to as its **1-hop neighbors**. The **2-hop neighbors** of a node v include all the neighbors of v's neighbors. For example, in the graph shown in Figure 3.2, the 1-hop neighbors of node 1 are {2, 4}. The 2-hop neighbors of node 1 include the neighbors of nodes 2 and 4, resulting in the set {2, 3, 4}. Some of these nodes, such as 2 and 4, also appear in the 1-hop neighborhood. While it's possible to exclude such duplicates, we include them in our definition. This concept can be extended to **k-hop neighbors**, where k is any natural number. Graph factorization methods typically use only the 1-hop neighborhood, whereas GraRep incorporates information from higher-hop neighborhoods. GraRep extends Graph Factorization by incorporating multi-step adjacency (k-hop neighbors) information to capture higher-order relationships in a graph. The closeness measure and loss function for GraRep are the same as for Graph Factorization.

For **similarity measure** in GraRep, instead of directly using the adjacency matrix A, we consider higher-order adjacency matrices A^K. This captures indirect connections between nodes up to k steps away:

$$S_G(v_i, v_j) = A_{ij}^K$$

Here, A^K is obtained by raising the adjacency matrix to the power of k, allowing the model to capture multi-hop connections.

Every k produces a d-dimensional embedding, which is then concatenated to produce the final embedding. Optimization at each k is done via singular value decomposition approximation. Embedding dimensions d and k are hyperparameters.

ACTIVITY

Download the Online Resources for this book and attempt **Programming Assignment 3.1.** It contains a detailed implementation of both of the embedding techniques discussed in this section for Zachary's Karate club network.

Attempting **Programming Assignment 3.1** at this stage will greatly enhance your understanding.

3.2 Random Walk-based Node Embedding

Methods discussed so far rely on deterministic similarity measures, some of which are difficult to scale for large graphs, such as computing A^K for large adjacency matrices. To address this, stochastic similarity-based methods have been proposed. The key idea is that nodes co-occurring in random walks of fixed length should be considered similar. This means that nodes frequently appearing together in a random walk should be mapped closer in the embedding space, allowing the model to capture both local and global graph structures more efficiently.

What is a random walk on a graph?

A random walk on a graph is a process where we start from a node and move to one of its neighboring nodes randomly at each step. From the new node, we again move to one of its neighbors. For a random walk of length *T*, we repeat this process *T* times.

> **EXAMPLE**
>
> Consider the graph in Figure 3.2. Let's perform a random walk of length 4 starting at node 2.
>
> 1. Start at node 2. The possible next nodes are 1, 3, or 4. Suppose we randomly pick 3.
> 2. At Node 3. The possible next nodes are 2 or 5. Suppose we randomly pick Node 5.
> 3. At Node 5. The only neighbor is Node 3, so we move back to Node 3.
> 4. At Node 3. The possible next nodes are 2 or 5. Suppose we pick Node 2.
>
> Thus, the random walk path is 2 → 3 → 5 → 3 → 2.

One could have also obtained a path 2 → 4 → 1 → 4 → 1. There are many such possibilities. Now, let's look at how node embeddings are generated using these random walks.

Node embeddings from random walks

In this approach, we first define two key parameters:

- **Walk length (*t*)**: The number of steps taken in a single random walk.
- **Number of walks per node (γ):** The number of random walks starting from each node.

For each node in the graph, we generate γ random walks of length t. These walks define a similarity measure between nodes based on how often they co-occur in walks. That is, if a node v frequently appears in walks starting from u $pG(v|u)$. Both t and γ are hyperparameters; generally, t takes integer values between 2 and 10.

In this scenario, the closeness measure (decoder function) is given by:

$$C(z_u, z_v) = \frac{\exp(z_u{}^T z_v)}{\sum_{n \in V} \exp(z_u{}^T z_n)}$$

And we expect $C(z_u, z_v) \approx p(v|u)$. To achieve this, we minimize the following loss function:

$$l = -\sum_{(v,u) \in D} \log(c(z_u, z_v))$$

where D is the set of node pairs (u, v) sampled from the random walks generated by the method above, i.e., $(u,v) \sim pG(v|u)$.

Let's look at the two most popular random walk-based embedding methods: DeepWalk and node2vec.

DeepWalk [Perozzi et al., 2014]

We can have different embedding techniques based on how random walks are generated. In DeepWalk, when standing at a node, we transition to any of its neighbors with equal probability. Look at the definition of closeness measure C for random walk-based methods; it involves a summation term in the denominator, which is computationally expensive. To address this, DeepWalk uses approximations to C. DeepWalk employs hierarchical softmax, a technique that accelerates probability calculations by structuring words (or nodes) in a hierarchical tree, reducing computation from linear to logarithmic complexity. The theoretical details of hierarchical softmax are skipped here, but can be found in *Perozzi et al. (2014)*. The PyTorch Geometric (PyG) implementation already incorporates these approximations.

> **ACTIVITY**
>
> Download the Online Resources for this book and attempt the **Programming Assignment 3.2**. It will guide you through implementing the Node2Vec algorithm using PyG, without needing to delve into the intricate theory.

Random walk for DeepWalk

In DeepWalk, standing at a node v, the probability of moving to node x is given by

$$p(w_i = x | w_{i-1} = v) = \begin{cases} 1/\deg(v) & \text{if } (v,x) \in E \\ 0 & \text{otherwise} \end{cases}$$

Node2Vec [Grover and Leskovec, 2016]

Node2Vec and DeepWalk differ in two key aspects: first, they have different methods to generate a random walk, and second, they use different approximations for C. In Node2Vec, the random walk is biased rather than uniform. The probability of moving closer to or farther from the starting node varies based on parameters, allowing the method to capture different types of node similarity. When the probability of returning to nearby nodes is high, the model emphasizes **homophily equivalence**, meaning highly interconnected nodes are mapped close together. Conversely, when the probability of moving away is high, the model captures **structural equivalence**, grouping nodes with similar roles rather than direct connections.

Another key difference from DeepWalk is that node2vec uses **negative sampling** (see *Grover and Leskovec, 2016*, for more details) instead of hierarchical softmax for efficient learning.

Random walk for Node2Vec

In node2vec, when starting at a node, the rule is the same as that of DeepWalk.

Figure 3.3 Random walk in node2vec

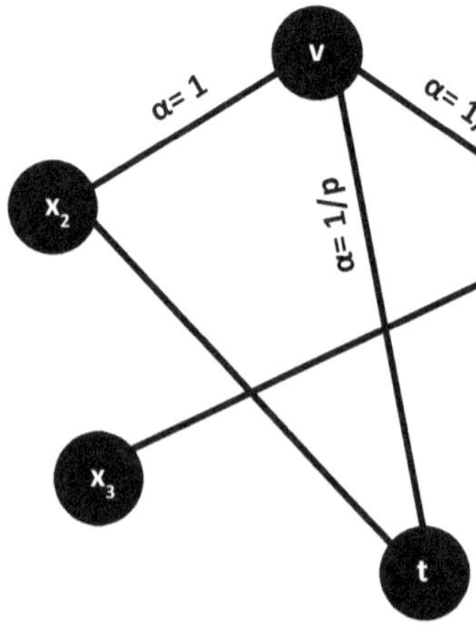

In the above graph, assuming we reached v from t, in node2vec standing at v, the probability of going back to t is proportional to 1/p, going to x_2 is proportional to 1, and going to x_1 is proportional to 1/q.

But after that, let's say you are standing at node v and you have come to v from node t, then the probability of moving to node x is given by (as shown in Figure 3.3)

$$p(w_i = x \mid w_{i-1} = v) = \begin{cases} \dfrac{\alpha_{pq}(t,x)}{\deg(v)} & \text{if } (v,x) \in E \\ 0 & \text{otherwise} \end{cases}$$

where

$$\alpha_{pq}(t,x) = \begin{cases} 1/p & if\ d_{tx} = 0 \\ 1 & if\ d_{tx} = 1 \\ 1/q & if\ d_{tx} = 2 \end{cases}$$

and d_{tx} is the shortest path distance between node t and x.

The **return parameter** p controls the likelihood of immediately revisiting a previously visited node in a random walk. Setting p to a high value ($p > max(q, 1)$) reduces the chance of revisiting nodes in the next two steps (unless there are no other neighbors to visit). This encourages moderate exploration while avoiding redundant 2-hop sampling. Conversely, a low p value ($p < min(q, 1)$) increases the likelihood of backtracking to the previously visited node, keeping the walk more localized around the starting node u.

The **in-out parameter** q determines whether the random walk is biased towards staying close to the last visited node or exploring farther regions of the graph. If $q > 1$, the walk favors nearby nodes, capturing a more localized view of the graph. In contrast, if $q < 1$, the walk prefers visiting nodes farther away, promoting a more exploratory behavior that encourages movement towards distant parts of the graph.

3.3 Edge Embedding

Once we have node embeddings, we can also create edge embeddings by combining the embeddings of the two nodes that form an edge. There are different ways to do this, and Table 3.1 lists some common methods. Just like node embeddings, edge embeddings can be used for tasks like link prediction or edge classification. The best way to combine node embeddings depends on the problem we are trying to solve and the structure of the graph.

Table 3.1 Different aggregations to obtain edge embedding from node embedding

Aggregation Operator	Definition
Average	$g_i(u,v)=\dfrac{f_i(u)+f_i(v)}{2}$
Hadamard	$g_i(u,v)=f_i(u)\times f_i(v)$
Weighted – L1	$g_i(u,v)=\lvert f_i(u)-f_i(v)\rvert$
Weighted – L2	$g_i(u,v)=\lvert f_i(u)-f_i(v)\rvert^2$

f(u) & *f(v)* denotes node embedding of *u* & *v*, respectively. The definitions correspond to the i-th component of edge embedding *g(u,v)*.

> **EXAMPLE**
>
> Let $f(u) = [2,3,4,1]$ and $f(v) = [1,0.5,2,2]$. Then, using Hadamard aggregation $g(u,v) = [2\times1,3\times0.5,4\times2,1\times2] = [2,1.5,8,2]$. Similarly, using Average aggregation $g(u,v) = [1.5,1.75,3,1]$.

3.4 Practical Insights on Using Graph Embedding

In this chapter, we explored various graph embedding techniques that map nodes to vectors in R^d, allowing us to apply traditional machine learning methods to graph-based problems. An important aspect of designing an embedding technique is the choice of similarity and closeness measures. While we discussed commonly used methods, one can design custom embeddings by selecting appropriate closeness measures such as cosine similarity, dot-product similarity, or Euclidean distance. Each measure captures different notions of similarity, and its effectiveness depends on the graph structure and the specific task. Euclidean distance is commonly used, but in high-dimensional spaces, it may not always be the best choice due to the curse of dimensionality. Cosine similarity, which measures the angle between vectors rather than their magnitude, is often preferred in applications where relative orientation matters more than absolute position, such as text and social network embeddings. Some methods also utilize dot-product similarity, which aligns well with models like matrix factorization-based approaches. The effectiveness of a particular distance metric depends on the structure of the graph and the nature of the task, making it an important consideration when designing graph embedding models.

Another key consideration in graph embeddings is the embedding dimension, which acts as a hyperparameter. Unlike traditional machine learning, where feature dimensions are often predefined, there is no widely accepted method to determine the optimal embedding dimension beforehand. Instead, it is typically tuned based on the dataset and application. Furthermore, there is no direct way to assess embedding quality just by visualizing the vectors; instead, performance on tasks like node classification is used to evaluate effectiveness. In the next chapter, we will explore deep learning-based approaches for graph learning, which extend these ideas further.

Chapter Summary

- Node embeddings allow us to represent graph nodes as fixed-length vectors, enabling the use of standard machine learning algorithms on graph data.
- A general embedding framework includes an encoder (embedding function), a similarity measure in the original graph, a closeness function in embedding space, and a loss function to align them.
- Matrix factorization methods like Graph Factorization and GraRep generate embeddings by decomposing adjacency-based matrices, with GraRep capturing multi-step (global) structure.
- Random walk–based methods like DeepWalk and Node2Vec learn embeddings by treating node sequences as sentences and applying language modeling techniques.
- Edge embeddings are computed by aggregating the embeddings of the two endpoint nodes, using operations such as concatenation or Hadamard product.
- Embedding dimension, closeness measure, and loss function are key design choices, and embeddings are typically evaluated through performance on downstream tasks like node classification or link prediction.

Quiz

1. **What is the primary motivation behind graph embedding?**
   a. To replace graphs with adjacency matrices
   b. To enable the use of traditional machine learning methods on graph-structured data
   c. To visualize graphs in two dimensions
   d. To remove the need for graph algorithms

2. **Which of the following is NOT a commonly used node similarity measure in graph embeddings?**
   a. Cosine similarity
   b. Dot-product similarity
   c. Manhattan distance
   d. Euclidean distance

3. **In random walk-based embedding methods like DeepWalk, how is node similarity captured?**
   a. By calculating the shortest path between nodes
   b. By counting the number of common neighbors
   c. By measuring the co-occurrence of nodes in random walks
   d. By directly using the adjacency matrix values

4. **What is the main difference between DeepWalk and Node2Vec?**
    a. Node2Vec uses uniform random walks, whereas DeepWalk uses biased walks
    b. DeepWalk uses uniform random walks, whereas Node2Vec introduces bias in walks
    c. DeepWalk uses hierarchical softmax, while Node2Vec uses matrix factorization
    d. Node2Vec does not generate embeddings, while DeepWalk does

5. **Which method does Node2Vec use to approximate the denominator in its closeness measure?**
    a. Hierarchical softmax
    b. Negative sampling
    c. Singular value decomposition
    d. Spectral clustering

6. **How are edge embeddings typically obtained from node embeddings?**
    a. By averaging node embeddings at both ends of an edge
    b. By summing the adjacency matrix rows corresponding to the edge
    c. By taking the Hadamard product of node embeddings
    d. Various aggregation methods can be used, depending on the application

7. **Which of the following is TRUE about evaluating graph embeddings?**
   a. The quality of an embedding can be judged by visualizing the vectors
   b. The performance of embeddings is assessed based on tasks like node classification
   c. Higher-dimensional embeddings always result in better performance
   d. Closeness measures are irrelevant in evaluating embeddings

Use the following information to answer Questions 8-10. **Edge Homophily:** it is the fraction of edges in the graph whose endpoints share the same label. Mathematically, it is defined as:

$$Edge\ Homophily = \frac{|\{(u,v) \in E \mid y(u) = y(v)\}|}{|E|}$$

8. **Calculate the Edge homophily of the following graphs:**

a. 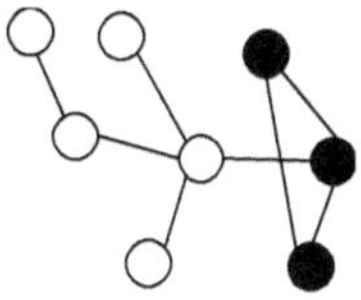

b. 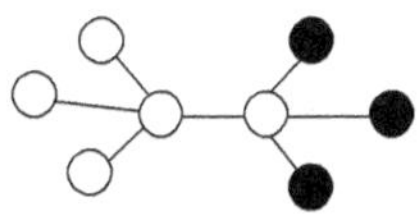

9. **Graphs with a high value of edge homophily (similar to (a)) are referred to as homophilic graphs. What values of *p* and *q* should one choose when working with homophilic graphs?**

10. Graphs with a low value of edge homophily (similar to (b)) are referred to as heterophilic graphs. What values of p and q should one choose when working with heterophilic graphs?

Answers

1 – b	2 – c	3 – c	4 – b	5 – b
6 – d	7 – b	8 – a) 0.875 b) 0.143	9 –	10 –

CHAPTER 4

Basics of Graph Neural Networks

Key Learning Objectives

- Understand the motivation for using Graph Neural Networks over earlier embedding techniques
- Learn the architecture and components of a basic GNN
- Explore common aggregation methods and their importance in message passing
- Comprehend the role of self-loops and normalization in GNN design
- Study the Graph Convolutional Network (GCN) architecture

In earlier chapters, we explored graph embedding techniques like matrix factorization and random walks. While these methods are useful, they often struggle to incorporate node features or generalize to unseen nodes. This chapter introduces **Graph Neural Networks (GNNs)**, a family of models that overcome these limitations by combining node features with graph structure using message passing. Methods like matrix factorization and random walk-based capture the structure of the graph quite well, but they fall short in some important ways. Take a social network graph, for example. Each node in the graph, representing a user, often comes with useful information like age, gender, location, and more. These features can be crucial for making predictions about the node. However, the embedding techniques we discussed earlier don't have a natural way to incorporate such node features. Another limitation is that they are transductive in nature—if a new node appears in the graph, we can't make predictions for it unless we recompute the embeddings for the entire graph.

One might consider using standard deep learning methods by feeding in node features, but these methods ignore the graph structure, which often leads to poor performance. What we need is a way to combine the power of node features with the structure of the graph.

This is where GNNs come in. GNNs are a class of models designed to work directly on graph-structured data. They learn from both the features of nodes and their local neighborhoods, making them powerful tools for a wide range of tasks. In this chapter, we'll introduce the basic concepts behind GNNs, explore their architecture, and understand how they bridge the gap between traditional deep learning and graph-based learning.

4.1 Multi-Layer Perceptron – A Quick Recap

Before diving into Graph Neural Networks, let's quickly revisit a commonly used neural network model: the **Multi-Layer Perceptron (MLP)**. An MLP is a type of neural network where the input features of a data point are passed through a series of layers to produce an output. As shown in Figure 4.1, it starts with an input layer, where the features are fed in. These features are then transformed step by step using matrix multiplications.

For example, the input vector i is first transformed into a hidden representation h^1 by multiplying it with a weight matrix W_1:

$$h^1 = W_1 i$$

This hidden representation is then further transformed:

$$h^2 = W_2 h^1$$

And finally, we get the output vector o:

$$o = W_3 h^2$$

The matrices W_1, W_2, W_3 are learned during training so that the model gives the correct output for most inputs. While this example uses two hidden layers, deeper networks can be used depending on the application.

If we generalize this process, and assume $h^0 = i$ (input) and $h^n = o$ (output), then we can write: $h^1 = W_l h^{l-1}$

More generally, in most neural networks, we can think of this transformation as: $h^1 =$ UPDATE (h^{l-1}) where **UPDATE** could be multiplying by a matrix, applying a non-linearity, or more complex rules depending on the model. The key takeaway is that MLPs update each data point independently—they don't consider the features or positions of other data points in the dataset. This becomes a major limitation when working with graphs, where the relationships between data points (nodes) are essential. In the next sections, we'll see how Graph Neural Networks address this. More details on MLPs are provided in Appendix A.

Figure 4.1 **Multi-Layer Perceptron Architecture**

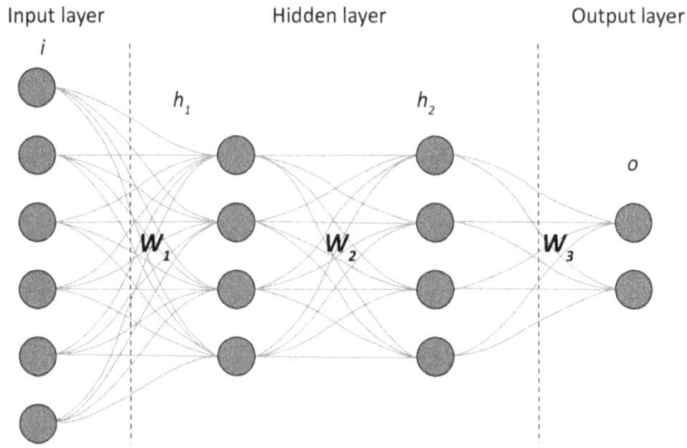

4.2 Introduction to Graph Neural Network

Just like in an MLP, in a Graph Neural Network (GNN), we also want to transform input features through a series of hidden layers into a final output. But there's a key difference: in GNNs, we update the feature representation of a node not only based on its own features, but also by using information from its neighbors.

Let's say h_v^l is the representation of node v at the l th layer. Then the update rule in a GNN can be written as:

$$h_v^l = UPDATE\left(h_v^{l-1}, AGGREGATE\left(\left\{h_u^{l-1} \mid u \in N(v)\right\}\right)\right) = UPDATE\left(h_v^{l-1}, m_{N(u)}^{l-1}\right)$$

Here's what's happening:

- **AGGREGATE:** This function collects information from the neighbors of node v and produces a combined message $m_{N(v)}^{l-1}$.
- **UPDATE:** This function takes both the current node's previous representation and the aggregated neighbor information to update the node's new representation.

While UPDATE is similar to what we've seen in traditional neural networks, the key difference here is that it now uses two inputs: the node's own features and the aggregated features from its neighbors.

Different GNN architectures use different kinds of AGGREGATE and UPDATE functions. The overall idea remains the same, but the way we combine and update information can vary. Before diving into examples, let's understand an important property that the AGGREGATE function must satisfy.

4.2.1 AGGREGATE Function

The AGGREGATE function combines the features of all the neighbors of a node into a single message vector. Since the neighbors of a node are naturally unordered (they form a **set**, not a sequence), the aggregation function must be **permutation-invariant**. That means it should give the same result no matter the order in which we provide the neighbor features.

For example, suppose node 1 has two neighbors, node 2 and node 3 (Figure 4.2). Then the aggregation should satisfy:

$$AGGREGATE\left(h_2^{l-1}, h_3^{l-1}\right) = AGGREGATE\left(h_3^{l-1}, h_2^{l-1}\right)$$

Common aggregation functions that naturally satisfy this property include: Sum, Average, and Max.

To make things concrete, let's look at a very simple example of a Graph Neural Network. In this example, the representation of a node v at layer l is updated as follows:

$$h_v^{1} = w_{l1} h_v^{l-1} + w_{l2}\left(\sum_{u \in N(v)} h_u^{l-1}\right)$$

In this case:

- The **AGGREGATE** function is simply the **sum** of the neighbors' representations.
- The **UPDATE** function is a **linear combination** of the node's own features and the aggregated neighbor features, using two separate weight matrices W_{l1} and W_{l2}. Both matrices are to be learnt during training. These matrices are generally used to change the dimensions of hidden representations.

This defines a very simple GNN with aggregate being sum and update being simple matrix multiplication. This overall approach of updating node representations using information from neighbors is commonly referred to as **message passing**. It is called so because, in each layer, nodes are essentially "sending" their representations as **messages** to their neighbors, which are then aggregated and used to update the receiving node's representation.

Figure 4.2 Pictorial representation of message passing algorithm

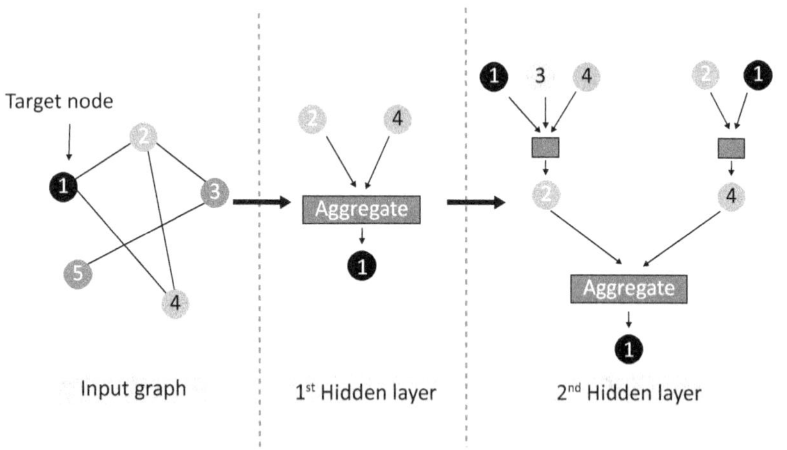

For the target node 1, in the first hidden layer, features from its neighbors—nodes 2 and 4—are aggregated. Simultaneously, for node 2, features from nodes 1, 3, and 4 are aggregated, and for node 4, features from nodes 1 and 2 are aggregated. In the second hidden layer, node 1 aggregates the updated features of nodes 2 and 4 obtained from the first layer.

4.2.2 Normalization in AGGREGATE function

Now that we understand the role of the AGGREGATE function in GNNs, let's look at some common techniques used to aggregate the features of a node's neighbors. We've already seen summation as a simple aggregation method. However, a challenge with this approach is that nodes with different degrees (i.e., different numbers of neighbors) will end up aggregating different numbers of feature vectors. As a result, the **aggregated message** m_v^l could have very different magnitudes across nodes, which can make optimization harder during training. One straightforward way to address this issue is **mean aggregation**, where we normalize the sum by dividing by the number of neighbors:

$$m_{N(v)}^l = \frac{\sum_{u \in N(v)} h_u^l}{|N(v)|}$$

This ensures that the scale of the aggregated message remains more consistent, regardless of the node's degree. Another popular approach is **symmetric normalization**, as used in the GCN model by Kipf and Welling (2016) (details about GCN are in Section 4.3.1). In this method, the neighbor features are scaled using both the degree of the central node and that of each neighbor:

$$m_{N(v)}^l = \sum_{u \in N(v)} \frac{h_u^l}{|N(v)|\,|N(u)|}$$

This normalization helps balance the influence of neighbors with different connectivity levels, making training more stable. Normalization in GNNs can sometimes obscure structural information, making it harder to distinguish nodes based on degree or graph position. Its usefulness depends on the task; normalization tends to help when node features carry more signal than the structure or when there's a wide variation in node degrees that could destabilize training. In contrast, for tasks that rely heavily on structural patterns, avoiding normalization may preserve important information.

We'll encounter more aggregation strategies in upcoming chapters when we study advanced GNN architectures. Similarly, we'll also explore different forms of UPDATE functions beyond the simple linear combinations we've seen so far in upcoming chapters.

4.3 Self-Loop-Based Methods

One way to simplify the GNN update rule is by including self-loops in the graph and absorbing the UPDATE step into the AGGREGATE step. A **self-loop** is an edge that connects a node to itself. By adding a self-loop to every node, we effectively include the node's own previous representation as part of its neighborhood. This allows us to define the update rule in a simplified form:

$$h_1^v = AGGREGATE\left(\left\{h_u^{l-1} \mid u \in N(v) U \{v\}\right\}\right)$$

This way, a node's own representation is treated the same as its neighbors', eliminating the need to define a separate update function. While this makes it easier to define and implement GNNs and may help reduce overfitting by lowering the number of parameters, it also comes with a drawback: it can reduce the model's expressiveness, since it no longer learns a distinct transformation for the node's own features.

4.3.1 Graph Convolutional Network (GCN)

The **Graph Convolutional Network (GCN)**, proposed by Kipf and Welling in 2016, is one of the most widely used GNN architectures. It builds on the ideas we've discussed so far by using **symmetric normalization** and including self-loops in the graph. The update rule for a node v in GCN is given by:

$$h_v^l : W_1 \sum_{u \in N(v)} \frac{h_u^{l-1}}{|N(u)|\,|N(v)|}$$

In practice, it's common to apply a **nonlinear activation function** (like ReLU) after the aggregation step to help the model learn more complex patterns. The modified update rule becomes:

$$h^l_{\ v} = \sigma\left(w_1 \sum_{u \in N(v)} \frac{h_u^{\ l-1}}{|N(u)|\,|N(v)|} \right)$$

Note: In libraries like PyTorch Geometric (PYG), the GCN layer implementation typically does not include the activation function, so it must be applied manually after the layer.

4.4 GNN for Node Classification

We've already discussed node classification in detail in earlier chapters. Now that we have introduced Graph Neural Networks, let's see how they can be applied to solve node classification tasks more effectively.

For a given node v, with an input feature vector h_v^0, we pass it through k layers of a GNN. After these layers, we obtain a new representation h_v^k, which is a learned embedding that captures both the node's features and the structure of its neighborhood.

This embedding can then be passed through a simple Multi-Layer Perceptron (MLP) to make the final prediction. If the task is to classify the node into one of the c classes, the final MLP output will be a vector of size c, which can be converted into a **probability distribution** over the classes using the **softmax function**:

$$y_v' = softmax(z_v) = \frac{exp(Z_v^i)}{\sum_{j=1}^{c} exp(Z_v^j)}$$

Here, z_v is the output from the MLP (or directly from the GNN, as discussed below), and y_v' is the predicted class probability distribution for node v.

Figure 4.3 Node classification using GNN

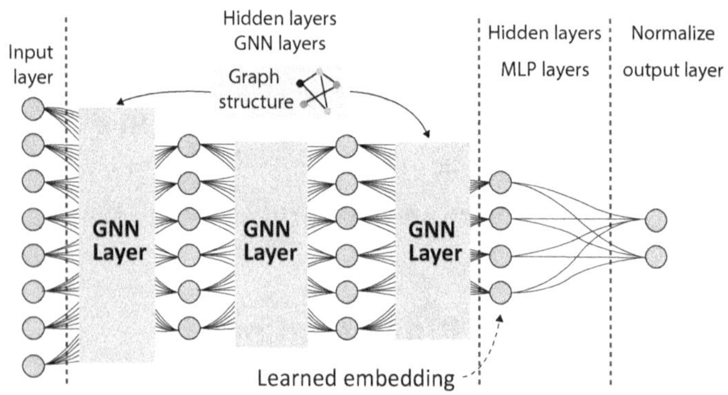

The input features are transformed into learned embeddings through a series of GNN layers. A simple MLP is then applied to these embeddings to produce an output layer, which is normalized (e.g., using softmax) to yield class probabilities. Observe that GNN layers require extra input (Graph structure), which is not used by the MLP layer.

To train the model, we compare the predicted probability distribution y_v' with the true class label using **cross-entropy**

loss. For a single labeled node v with ground truth label y_v, the loss is:

$$L_v = -\sum_{c=1}^{C} y_v[c] \log(y'_v[c])$$

The total loss is calculated over all training nodes, typically using:

$$L = \frac{1}{|D_{train}|} \sum_{v \in D_{train}} L_v$$

Note: In Pytorch, different loss functions behave differently with respect to the softmax operation:

- torch.nn.CrossEntropyLoss expects raw logits (unnormalized outputs), and it applies log_softmax internally.
- torch.nn.NLLLoss (negative log-likelihood) expects log-probabilities (e.g., obtained by applying log_ softmax manually).

Make sure to choose the appropriate format for your model's output based on the loss function you're using.

While it is common to pass the final node embeddings through an MLP, it is not always necessary. In fact, the last GNN layer can be designed such that the output embedding dimension is equal to the number of classes. In such cases, the output can be directly passed through a softmax function to obtain probabilities, without any MLP.

During training, only the embeddings of labeled nodes are used to compute the loss and update the weights. However, in most GNN models, all nodes in the graph contribute to the forward pass due to the message-passing nature of GNNs—even if they are not labeled.

ACTIVITY

Download the Online Resources for this book and attempt **Programming Assignment 4.1**. It includes exercises for the implementation of GNN for node classification.

Chapter Summary

- Graph Neural Networks (GNNs) extend traditional neural networks to graph-structured data by aggregating information from a node's neighborhood.
- The core operation in a GNN involves two key functions: AGGREGATE, which collects messages from neighbors, and UPDATE, which combines them with the node's own representation.
- Aggregation functions must be permutation invariant to handle unordered sets of neighbors; common methods include sum, mean, and normalized aggregation.
- Introducing self-loops simplifies the update rule and allows a node's own features to be included in its updated representation.
- The Graph Convolutional Network (GCN) is a widely used GNN variant that incorporates symmetric normalization and self-loops in its design.
- For node classification tasks, GNNs are followed by a classification layer (often an MLP), and training is done using cross-entropy loss applied to the final output layer.

Quiz

1. **In GNNs, what is the primary difference between how traditional neural networks and GNNs update a node's representation?**
   a. Traditional NNs use edge features; GNNs do not
   b. GNNs update a node based on its own and its neighbors' features
   c. GNNs ignore the structure of the data
   d. Traditional NNs use message passing

2. **Which of the following functions is not permutation invariant?**
   a. Sum
   b. Mean
   c. Max
   d. Concatenation in input order

3. **Which of the following is not a desirable property of the AGGREGATE function?**
   a. Permutation invariance
   b. Differentiability
   c. Scalability
   d. Dependency on neighbor order

4. **What does permutation invariance mean in the context of GNNs?**
   a. Node features must be sorted
   b. Graphs should be complete
   c. The output should remain the same regardless of the order of neighbors
   d. The loss function must be symmetric

5. **Recall the definition of Heterophilic graphs mentioned in Question 9 of the Quiz in Chapter 3. Would GCN be useful for a heterophilic graph? If yes, why? If not, why not?**

6. **How can you modify GCN to be useful for Heterophilic graphs?**

7. **Why are self-loops often added to graphs before applying GNNs?**
   a. To convert them into trees
   b. To prevent overfitting
   c. To include a node's own features during aggregation
   d. To reduce graph diameter

8. **Which statement best describes a Graph Convolutional Network (GCN)?**
   a. A type of recurrent network on graphs
   b. A GNN with a dot-product decoder
   c. A GNN that uses symmetric normalization and self-loops
   d. A pooling-based node classifier

9. **The representation of a node after multiple GNN layers is expected to capture:**
   a. Only its own features
   b. Noisy information
   c. Information from its neighborhood
   d. Random graph statistics

10. **What would happen if an aggregation function is not permutation invariant?**
    a. GNN will ignore the graph structure
    b. Model performance might vary depending on node ordering
    c. The GNN will underfit
    d. It prevents the use of node features

Answers

1 – b	2 – d	3 – d	4 – c
5 – GCN's feature smoothing causes information mixing between dissimilar nodes, so node representations lose discriminative power.			
6 – Open-ended question.			
7 – c	8 – c	9 – c	10 – b

CHAPTER 5

GNN for Edge Prediction and Graph Classification

Key Learning Objectives

- Understanding how GNNs can be used for edge prediction tasks, such as link prediction
- Learning how to construct edge embeddings using pooled node embeddings
- Exploring the working of Graph AutoEncoder (GAE) and its loss formulation
- Understanding subgraph-based link prediction using SEAL and DRNL labeling
- Applying GNNs to graph classification tasks using mean, sum, and attention-based pooling
- Learning how attention and node selection work in Self-Attention Graph Pooling (SAGPool)

In this chapter, we explore how Graph Neural Networks (GNNs) can be applied to two important graph-level tasks: **edge prediction** and **graph classification**. These tasks are central to a wide range of real-world applications, from recommending new connections in social networks to classifying entire molecular graphs in drug discovery.

The chapter is divided into two main sections:

1. **GNN for Edge Prediction**
2. **GNN for Graph Classification**

For both tasks, we will begin with simple but effective pooling-based methods, which are easy to implement and perform well in many practical scenarios. These methods act as a solid foundation and are often sufficient for prototyping or solving moderately complex problems. We will then move on to more sophisticated techniques, which offer improved performance at the cost of added complexity. These advanced methods are presented as optional tools for readers working on challenging applications where basic methods fall short.

The goal of this chapter is to equip you with a practical understanding of how to structure and train GNNs for these two tasks while giving you the flexibility to choose the right level of complexity for your specific use case.

5.1 GNN for Edge Prediction

We have already discussed heuristic algorithms for edge prediction in Chapter 2 and embedding-based methods in Chapter 3. In this section, we'll explore how to use **Graph Neural Networks** to perform the same task in a more flexible and learnable way.

5.1.1 Simple pooling-based method

The core idea is simple: once we've obtained node embeddings (i.e., node-level feature representations after k rounds of GNN message passing), we can combine the embeddings of two nodes to form an **edge embedding**. This edge embedding is then passed through a small **MLP** to predict a score for that edge, typically representing the likelihood of the edge existing.

There are various ways to aggregate the node embeddings to form an edge embedding. Techniques like sum, Hadamard product, and others, as discussed in Table 3.1, can be used here. These methods are simple, efficient, and serve as straightforward extensions of the GNN pipeline to edge-level prediction.

5.1.2 Graph AutoEncoder

The **Graph AutoEncoder (GAE)**, proposed by Kipf and Welling 2016, is one of the simplest and most elegant frameworks for edge prediction using GNNs. In this approach, node representations z_i are learned using a **Graph Convolutional Network (GCN)**.

Once the node embeddings are obtained, a **score** for the presence of an edge between any two nodes i and j is computed using the inner product of their embeddings, followed by a sigmoid activation:

$$A^*_{\{ij\}} = \sigma(z_i^T z_j)$$

Here A^* is the predicted adjacency matrix, and σ is the sigmoid function that maps the score to a probability between 0 and 1.

The model is trained to minimize the binary cross-entropy loss between the true adjacency matrix A and the predicted matrix A^*:

$$L = -[A_{ij}\log(A^*_{ij}) + (1 - A_{ij})\log(1 - A^*_{ij})]$$

In real-world graphs, the number of positive edges (i.e., existing connections) is usually much smaller than the number of negative edges (i.e., node pairs without an edge).

To address this class imbalance, it's common to **upweight the loss** terms corresponding to positive edges during training. This ensures that the model doesn't become biased toward predicting negatives due to their overwhelming majority.

5.1.3 Subgraph-based methods: SEAL

While approaches like Graph AutoEncoder rely on global node embeddings, another powerful idea is to focus only on the local structure around the target edge. This is the key idea behind **SEAL** (Subgraph Embedding-based Link prediction), proposed by Zhang and Chen in 2018.

The SEAL method works by first extracting a **local subgraph** around each target edge, that is, the edge we want to predict. Typically, this involves collecting a fixed-size neighborhood (e.g., all nodes within 2 hops) around the two nodes and whose connection we're evaluating.

Once the subgraph is extracted, it is treated as a small graph on its own. Node features in this subgraph are constructed based on structural roles, for instance, which nodes are i, j, or how close a node is to them in terms of the shortest path. Instead of using the original node features (which may not always be available or informative), SEAL constructs structural role-based features for the nodes in the subgraph. A common approach is **Double-Radius Node Labeling (DRNL)**, which assigns each node a label based on its distance to the two target nodes u and v. These features help the model understand the position and importance of each node in the local context.

Then, instead of using a GNN on the full graph, a GNN is trained on each extracted subgraph to predict whether the target edge should exist. The GNN learns patterns in the structure of local neighborhoods that are indicative of the presence or absence of a link.

SEAL is especially useful in cases where local topology holds strong signals about edge formation, like social networks or citation graphs, and it allows for learning rich, task-specific features without relying on global node embeddings.

Constructing features using DRNL

In subgraph-based link prediction methods like SEAL, we work with small subgraphs extracted around the target edge (u,v). To make the GNN effective on these subgraphs, we need a way to represent the role each node plays in the structure. One popular technique for this is Double-Radius Node Labeling (DRNL). DRNL assigns each node in the subgraph a label based on how close it is to the two nodes u and v, the endpoints of the edge we are trying to predict. Specifically, for any node x, it computes:

- $d_1 = dist(x,u)$: The shortest path distance from x to u
- $d_2 = dist(x,v)$: The shortest path distance from x to v

These two distances are then combined into a single integer label using a simple rule designed to distinguish structural roles. The **closed-form formula** used in the original SEAL paper to compute the label is:

$$DRNL(x) = 1 + \min(d_1, d_2) + \left[\frac{d_1 + d_2}{2}\right]\left(\left[\frac{d_1 + d_2}{2}\right] + (d_1 + d_2) \bmod 2 - 1\right)$$

This formula assigns lower labels to nodes that are more "central" in the subgraph with respect to u and v, and higher labels to more peripheral nodes. Importantly, this **perfect hashing** ensures that nodes with different distance combinations get unique and meaningful labels. The two target nodes themselves, u and v, are usually assigned a fixed label (often 1), so they are clearly identifiable by the model.

Once each node has been assigned a label, we convert the label into a one-hot encoded vector, a common method of turning categorical data into numerical input suitable for neural networks. This gives us a feature representation that encodes the position of each node in the subgraph relative to the edge of interest.

Combining DRNL with original features

In many real-world graphs, nodes come with their own features, such as age, type, or description. These original features can carry important information, so instead of using only DRNL-based features, we concatenate the two:

Final Node Feature = [Orginal Features | | DRNL One-Hot Label]

This combined feature vector gives the model access to both **Structural role** information from DRNL and **Node-specific attributes** from the original graph.

This enriched representation is then used as the input to a GNN, typically a few layers deep, which operates on the extracted subgraph to generate a prediction for whether the edge (u,v) should exist.

> **ACTIVITY**
>
> Download the online resources for this book and attempt **Programming Assignment 5.1**. It covers edge prediction via GNNs and will help you apply what you just learned.

5.2 GNN for Graph Classification

In the previous section, we saw how GNNs can be used for node-level and edge-level prediction tasks. In this section, we shift our focus to graph-level tasks, where the goal is to assign a label or make a prediction for the entire graph rather than its individual components.

5.2.1 Simple Pooling-Based Method

After applying a GNN to a graph, we obtain an embedding (i.e., a feature vector) for each node. To use these node-level embeddings for graph-level classification, we need a way to combine them into a single vector that represents the whole graph. This is where pooling functions come in.

A pooling function takes all node embeddings in a graph and aggregates them into a single vector. The simplest and most commonly used pooling functions are Sum pooling, Mean (average) pooling, Max pooling, and Min pooling. These functions are applied component-wise; that is, each dimension of the final graph-level embedding is computed by aggregating the corresponding dimensions of all node embeddings.

For example, the mean pooling operation for a graph *G* having nodes, with node embeddings $\{h_1, h_2, \ldots, h_n\}$ produces the graph embedding h_G as:

$$h_G = \frac{1}{n}\sum_{i=1}^{n} h_i$$

Here, *n* is the number of nodes in the graph, and $h_i \in R^d$ is the embedding of node *i*. The output $h_G \in R^d$ has the same dimensionality as the node embeddings and represents the entire graph in a fixed-size vector. These simple pooling methods are efficient and often perform surprisingly well in many graph classification tasks.

5.2.2 Attention-Based Pooling Layer

While simple pooling methods like mean or sum treat all nodes equally during aggregation, they may not always capture the most important parts of a graph. In many real-world graphs, some nodes are more relevant than others for making a prediction. For example, in a molecular graph, in hydrocarbon-based molecules, small groups of atoms known as functional groups, like a hydroxyl group (–OH) or a carboxyl group (–COOH), can drastically affect the molecule's properties, such as acidity or reactivity, even though the rest of the molecule may consist of similar carbon and hydrogen chains. In such cases, hydrogen atoms on the outer carbon atoms may contribute very little to the property of interest. Giving equal weight to all atoms can therefore dilute the influence of these important substructures, leading to less meaningful graph-level representations. Also, for instance, in a social network graph predicting the likelihood of a rumor spreading, highly connected users (e.g., influencers or community leaders) play a disproportionately large role compared to low-activity users. Pooling all nodes with equal weight could overlook the influence of these central nodes and lead to inaccurate predictions.

To address this, **attention-based pooling** techniques assign **different importance weights to different nodes** before aggregating their embeddings. These weights are learned during training, allowing the model to **focus on the most relevant nodes** in the graph for the given task.

Let's say $h_1, h_2, \ldots, h_n \in R^d$ are the node embeddings. Attention-based pooling computes a weight α_i for each node embedding h_i, and the final graph embedding is computed as a **weighted sum**:

$$h_G = \sum_{i=1}^{n} \alpha_i h_i$$

The attention weights α_i are learned by the model and typically computed using a small neural network (or even a dot-product attention mechanism). These weights are normalized using a **softmax function** so that they sum to 1:

$$\alpha_i = \frac{\exp\left(w^T \tanh(h_i)\right)}{\sum_{j=1}^{n} \exp\left(w^T \tanh(h_j)\right)}$$

Here, $w \in R^d$ is a learnable parameter vector, and the tanh activation helps introduce non-linearity. The softmax ensures the weights form a valid probability distribution.

This approach allows the model to dynamically decide which nodes to pay more attention to, depending on the structure and features of the input graph. In practice, attention-based pooling often improves performance on complex graph classification tasks by making the aggregation process more adaptive.

5.2.3 SAGPool: Self-Attention Graph Pooling

SAGPool (Self-Attention Graph Pooling), introduced by Lee et al. (2019), is a special type of attention-based pooling that not only weighs node importance but also selects a subset of important nodes, rather than aggregating all of them. This makes it especially useful when we want to reduce the size of the graph while retaining its most informative parts.

In SAGPool, each node is first passed through a standard GNN layer to obtain its embedding h_v. Then, instead of treating all node embeddings equally, SAGPool computes a self-attention score for each node using a learnable parameter vector $\theta_{att} \in R^{d\times 1}$, where d is the dimension of the node embeddings. The attention score for node v is computed as:

$$Z(v) = \sigma(h_v) \cdot \theta_{att}$$

Here, h_v is the node embedding of node v, obtained from a GNN layer, Θ_{att} is a learnable vector, and σ is a nonlinear activation function (like ReLU or tanh). The dot product gives a scalar score indicating the importance of node v.

Once the attention scores $Z(v)$ are calculated for all nodes in the graph, only the top-k scoring nodes (based on a fixed ratio like 50%) are retained. The rest are discarded, along with their edges. The remaining subgraph is then used as input to the next GNN layer or passed to the final classifier.

ACTIVITY

Download the online resources for this book and attempt **Programming Assignment 5.2**. It includes Graph Classification using GNN and will help you apply what you learned in this section.

Chapter Summary

- Graph Neural Networks can be extended to edge-level tasks like link prediction by aggregating node embeddings to form edge embeddings, which are then used to predict the presence of an edge.
- Graph AutoEncoders (GAE) learn node embeddings through a GNN and reconstruct the graph's adjacency matrix using a similarity function; training is done via cross-entropy loss.
- SEAL (Subgraph Embedding-based Link Prediction) predicts edges by extracting local enclosing subgraphs around candidate edges and labeling nodes using structural encodings like DRNL, which are combined with original features.
- For graph-level tasks such as graph classification, node embeddings are aggregated into a single graph embedding using simple pooling methods like mean, sum, or max.
- Attention-based pooling techniques weigh node contributions differently based on learned importance scores, allowing the model to focus on more informative nodes.
- Advanced pooling approaches like SAGPool integrate self-attention within GNN layers to select and retain the most relevant nodes during pooling, enhancing graph classification performance.

Quiz

1. In the Graph AutoEncoder framework, what does the predicted adjacency matrix A^* represent?
2. True/ False. In real-world graphs, the number of positive edges is often greater than the number of negative edges.
3. What is the most common loss function used in Graph AutoEncoders for edge prediction?
   a. Mean squared error
   b. Cross-entropy loss
   c. Hinge loss
   d. Contrastive loss
4. Explain why positive edges may be upweighted during training in edge prediction tasks.
5. Given two nodes i and j, and their GCN-derived embeddings z_i and z_j, how is the score for predicting an edge between them computed in GAE?
6. Given $d(i,x)=2$, $d(i,y)=3$, compute the DRNL label $DRNL(i)$ using the closed-form expression.
7. In attention-based pooling, why is a softmax function used when computing the weights?
8. Explain how the self-attention score in SAGPool is computed from a GNN layer's output.

9. **Which of the following is NOT a common method for aggregating node embeddings to form an edge embedding?**
   - **a.** Sum pooling
   - **b.** Hadamard product
   - **c.** Matrix inversion
   - **d.** Concatenation

10. **Explain why class imbalance is a challenge in edge prediction tasks and how the Graph AutoEncoder (GAE) addresses it.**

Solutions:

1. $A^{*}_{\{ij\}} = \sigma(z_i^T z_j)$
2. False
3. b
4. Positive edges are often **upweighted** because they are **fewer than negative edges**, helping the model avoid bias toward predicting non-edges and improving learning on true connections.
5. In a Graph Autoencoder (GAE), the edge score between nodes *i* and *j* is computed as the dot product of their embeddings:

   $$\text{score } (i,j) = \sigma(z_i^{T} z_j)$$

   where σ is the sigmoid function.
6. 7
7. In attention-based pooling, the softmax is used to convert raw attention scores into positive weights that sum to 1, ensuring each node's contribution is normalized and comparable across the graph.
8. The attention score for node v is computed as:

   $$Z(v) = \sigma(h_v) \cdot \theta_{att}$$

   Here, h_v is the node embedding of node v, obtained from a GNN layer, Θ_{att} is a learnable vector, and σ is a nonlinear activation function (like ReLU or tanh). The dot product gives a scalar score indicating the importance of node v.
9. c
10. c

CHAPTER 6

Advanced GNN Architectures

Key Learning Objectives

- Understand the limitations of basic aggregation functions such as sum and mean in GNNs
- Explain how set pooling generalizes these functions using learnable transformations
- Describe how attention-based aggregation enables nodes to assign different levels of importance to different neighbors
- Define the oversmoothing problem and explain how it affects deep GNNs
- Identify and apply different strategies to mitigate oversmoothing, including: Concatenation-based updates, Skip connections, and Jumping Knowledge Networks

In Chapter 4, we introduced the idea of Graph Neural Networks (GNNs) and saw how they help us learn from both the features of a node and the structure of the graph around it. We learned that every GNN layer has two key steps:

1. **AGGREGATE:** gather information from the node's neighbors
2. **UPDATE:** use that information to update the node's own representation

Together, these steps allow each node to improve its understanding of the graph by "listening" to its neighborhood. To recap, the general update rule in a GNN looks like this:

$$h_v^l = UPDATE\left(h_v^{l-1}, AGGREGATE\left(\left\{h_u^{l-1} \mid u \in N(v)\right\}\right)\right) = UPDATE\left(h_v^l, m_{N(v)}^l\right)$$

In simple terms, each node updates itself by collecting messages from its neighbors. The formula above gives a general idea, but how we aggregate and update makes a big difference in how powerful and useful a GNN is. In this chapter, we'll look at advanced ways of doing both aggregating and updating the representation. These improvements help GNNs work better on real-world problems, especially when graphs are large, complex, or noisy.

6.1 Advanced Aggregation Methods

Let's begin by taking a closer look at aggregation. In Chapter 4, we discussed simple aggregation methods like summation, mean, and symmetric normalization. These methods are efficient and work well in many cases, but they treat all neighbors equally and rely on fixed mathematical operations. Instead of relying on such fixed rules, we now turn to more flexible and powerful approaches for aggregation.

In this section, we explore two such approaches: set pooling, which treats the neighborhood as an unordered set and applies learnable transformations to its elements, and neighborhood-based attention, which allows the model to assign different levels of importance to different neighbors during aggregation.

6.1.1 Set Pooling

Common aggregation functions like sum and mean encountered in Chapter 4 are examples of set aggregation functions. These functions take an unordered set of neighbor representations and return a single combined vector. They are called *set* functions because they treat the neighborhood as a set rather than a list, meaning the order of neighbors doesn't matter. This property is important because, in most graphs, there is no natural or meaningful order among the neighbors of a node.

While the sum and the mean are fast and easy to compute, they are also quite limited in how they combine information. They apply the same simple rule regardless of the content of the neighbor features or the graph structure. This raises an important question: *can we learn better ways to aggregate neighbor information, rather than fixing the rule in advance?*

Set pooling offers one such solution. The key idea is to allow the model to learn how to process each neighbor's features before combining them. A common approach is to pass each neighbor feature through a small neural network (such as a multilayer perceptron, or MLP), and then combine the results using a permutation-invariant function like sum, mean, or max, and then again pass through an MLP. Formally, we can write set pooling as follows:

$$m_{N(v)} = POOL\left(\left\{MLP_{\phi}h_u \mid u \in N(v)\right\}\right)$$

$$h_v^l = MLP_{\theta}(m_{N(v)})$$

Here:

- h_u is the feature vector of neighbor u,
- MLP is a small neural network that transforms each neighbor's feature,

- θ and ϕ are learnable parameters of MLP.
- POOL is a function like sum or max that combines all the transformed vectors into one.

By learning the transformation step (through the MLP), the model becomes more expressive. For example, it can learn to emphasize certain patterns or suppress noisy features, things a simple sum cannot do. In practice, this setup allows each neighbor to be "interpreted" differently depending on its content, before being merged with others.

This framework of applying a function to each element and then aggregating is not just a heuristic—it's also supported by theory. It has been shown that this type of structure can approximate any function over sets, as long as the MLP is powerful enough. This means that, in principle, set pooling can learn very complex aggregation strategies, all while respecting the unordered nature of the neighborhood.

In real-world models, the MLP used for set pooling is usually kept shallow, often just one or two layers, to reduce the risk of overfitting and keep the computation efficient. Set pooling bridges a gap between fixed aggregation rules and more flexible, learnable strategies. It retains the important property of permutation invariance while allowing the model to learn richer representations from local neighborhoods.

6.1.2 Neighbourhood-Based Attention

In all the aggregation methods we have seen so far, whether it is sum, mean, or even set pooling, one thing remains the same: every neighbor contributes equally or is processed in the same way. However, in many real-world graphs, this is rarely ideal. Not all neighbors are equally useful. Some may carry relevant information, while others might be noisy, misleading, or even irrelevant for the task.

To address this, attention-based aggregation allows the model to learn how much importance to assign to each neighbor. Instead of treating all neighbors identically, the model learns a weight for each one and combines their features accordingly. This way, more informative neighbors are given higher importance, and less useful ones contribute less.

This idea was introduced in **Graph Attention Networks (GAT)** by **Veličković et al. (2018)**. The model computes attention weights between a node and each of its neighbors and then uses these weights to perform a weighted sum of the neighbors' features:

$$m_{N(v)} = \sum_{u \in N(v)} \alpha_{vu} \cdot h_u$$

Here, h_u is the feature vector of neighbor u, and α_{vu} is the attention weight that reflects how important neighbor u is when updating node v. The attention weights are computed using a small neural network that looks at the features of both the target node and each of its neighbors. A simple way to compute the attention between node v and one of its neighbors u is:

$$\alpha_{vu} = \frac{\exp(a^T[Wh_v \,||\, Wh_u])}{\sum_{u' \in N(v)} \exp(a^T[Wh_v \,||\, Wh_{u'}])}$$

In this expression:

- W is a learnable weight matrix that transforms the node features
- a is a learnable vector
- || denotes the concatenation of the two feature vectors

However, in the original GAT model, a **nonlinear activation** was applied before computing the softmax. Specifically, the inner product $a^T[Wh_v || Wh_u]$ is first passed through a

LeakyReLU activation with a small negative slope (typically 0.2). This leads to weight

$$\alpha_{vu} = \frac{\exp(LeakyRelu(a^T[Wh_v \,||\, Wh_u]))}{\sum_{u' \in N(v)} \exp(LeakyRelu(a^T[Wh_v \,||\, Wh_{u'}]))}$$

This nonlinearity helps stabilize training and improves the model's ability to learn meaningful attention scores. The softmax function ensures that all the weights sum to one, turning the aggregation into a weighted average.

While GAT uses this specific form, the idea of neighborhood attention is more general. There are other ways to compute attention scores. For example:

- **Bilinear attention**, where the score between two nodes is computed as $h_v^T W h_{u'}$, using a learned weight matrix W.
- **MLP-based attention**, where the pair of features (h_v, h_u) is passed into a multilayer perceptron that returns a scalar score.

In both cases, these raw scores are passed through a softmax function, just like in GAT, to produce the normalized attention weights α_{vu}. This ensures that all the attention weights for a given node add up to one and can be interpreted as relative importance during aggregation. In all these cases, the goal remains the same: assign a meaningful weight to each neighbor based on its interaction with the target node. These weights are then used in a weighted average to produce the aggregated message.

6.1.3 Graph Transformers

The Transformer model was originally proposed for machine translation tasks in natural language processing. Its main idea is to use an attention mechanism that allows each word in a sentence to attend to every other word. This design makes it easy for the model to capture long-range relationships in text. Since then, Transformers have been widely adopted in other fields, including computer vision and, more recently, graph learning.

Extending Transformers to graphs is a natural step. The basic idea is similar to the neighborhood-based attention mechanism we discussed earlier, where nodes assign different importance to their neighbors during aggregation. However, Graph Transformers go beyond this by using multi-head attention, which allows each node to process its neighborhood in multiple different ways at the same time.

To understand this, we first need to explain what an attention head is. In simple terms, an attention head is a separate branch of the attention mechanism. Each head independently computes its own set of attention weights and aggregates information from the neighbors based on those weights.

Why use multiple heads? The key reason is that different attention heads can focus on different patterns in the neighborhood. For example, one head may learn to focus on nodes with similar features, while another head may focus on structurally important nodes like hubs or boundary nodes. By combining these different perspectives, the model becomes more expressive and better able to capture complex relationships within the graph.

In Graph Transformers, the aggregation process with multi-head attention can be described as follows. First, each head independently aggregates information from the neighbors:

$$a_k = W_k \sum_{u \in N(v)} \alpha_{v.u}^{(k)} h_u$$

Here:

- a_k is the output of the k-th attention head,
- W_k is a learnable weight matrix for the k-th head,
- $\alpha_{v,u}^{(k)}$ is the attention weight between node and neighbor for the k-th head, computed using a softmax function.

After all heads have processed the neighborhood, their outputs are combined, usually by concatenation:

$$m_{N(v)} = [a_1 \,||\, a_2 \,||\, \cdots \,||\, a_k]$$

This combined message is then passed to the update function to produce the new node representation. Graph Transformers offer a powerful and flexible way to aggregate information in graphs. By using multiple attention heads and allowing attention to adapt to the graph structure, these models can capture more complex patterns than many traditional GNNs. They have been successfully applied in areas such as molecular property prediction, protein interaction networks, and recommendation systems.

6.2 Advanced Update Function

In a Graph Neural Network, each layer updates a node's representation based on information gathered from its neighbors. At the first layer, a node aggregates features from its immediate neighbors and updates its own features. This means that after the first layer, the node carries information from all nodes directly connected to it.

When we apply a second GNN layer, each node again aggregates messages from its neighbors, but now those neighbors already contain information from their own neighbors. As a result, the second layer lets each node indirectly receive information from nodes that are two hops away (See Figure 4.2). Extending this idea, a GNN with k layers allows each node to access information from its $k-$ hop neighborhoods.

This is a powerful idea, but it comes with a downside. In many real-world graphs, such as social networks, citation graphs, and recommendation graphs, most nodes are not very far apart. Often, any two nodes are connected by paths of length 7 or 8 at most. So if we stack too many layers, information from almost every node starts to flow into every other node. As a result, the features of all nodes begin to look very similar. This is called the **oversmoothing effect**.

When oversmoothing happens, the model loses the ability to distinguish between nodes based on their features because everyone ends up with nearly the same representation. This makes it difficult to perform any downstream task, such as classification, because there is no meaningful difference left to learn from.

The choice of update function plays an important role in how we handle this problem. With the right design, we can allow the network to gather useful information from multiple hops without collapsing all representations into the same space. In the rest of this section, we will explore a few update strategies that help tackle oversmoothing. These include simple techniques like concatenating features across layers, as well as more structured solutions such as skip connections, gated updates, and jumping knowledge networks.

6.2.1 Concatenation-based updates

One simple yet effective way to deal with oversmoothing is to preserve more of the node's earlier representations as we move deeper into the network. Instead of replacing the old feature at every layer with a new one, we can keep both by concatenating them.

In this approach, after aggregating messages from the neighbors, we concatenate the node's previous feature vector with the aggregated message before applying the update function. The idea is that this combined input allows the model to preserve the local identity of the node (from the earlier layer) while also incorporating new information from the neighborhood.

The update rule becomes:

$$h_v^l = \sigma(W \cdot [h_v^{l-1} \,||\, m_{N(v)}^l])$$

Here, || denotes concatenation, $m_{N(v)}^l$ is the aggregated message from neighbors at layer l, and W is a learnable matrix that mixes the combined features. This formulation ensures that the previous state of the node is explicitly passed into the next layer, preventing it from being overwritten too quickly. Concatenation has a stabilizing effect, especially when the network is deep. It helps avoid losing the original signal too early, which is one of the causes of oversmoothing. However, one drawback is that it increases the dimensionality of the feature vectors at each layer, which can lead to higher memory and computation costs if not managed carefully.

6.2.2 Skip Connections

Skip connections offer another simple and widely used method to preserve information across layers. Instead of replacing the previous representation with the new one, we add them together. This technique comes from deep learning models like ResNets, where skip connections help avoid the vanishing gradient problem and allow deeper networks to train more reliably.

In the context of GNNs, a skip connection updates the node's representation by combining the new information from the neighbors with the old feature using element-wise addition:

$$h_v^l = \sigma(W.[h_v^{l-1} \,||\, m_{N(v)}^l]) + h_v^{l-1}$$

This simple addition ensures that the original node feature is retained at each layer, preventing the network from drifting too far away from the initial input. It also makes it easier for the model to learn identity mappings when needed, which helps reduce oversmoothing. An alternative form is to apply the transformation to both the old and new features before adding them:

$$h_v^l = \sigma(W_1.h_v^{l-1} + W_2.m_{N(v)}^l)$$

Here, the network learns how much to trust the previous state and how much to trust the new message from neighbors by using two separate weight matrices. Skip connections have become a default design choice in many GNN architectures, especially when the number of layers increases. They are simple to implement and often help with both training stability and model performance.

6.2.3 Gated Updates*

The idea of using gates to control information flow comes from sequence models in natural language processing, such as GRUs and LSTMs. In those models, gates decide how much of the past should be remembered and how much of the new input should be accepted at each step.

The same idea can be applied to Graph Neural Networks across layers. Rather than fully replacing the node's feature at every layer, gated update functions allow the network to learn how much of the previous representation to retain and how much of the new aggregated message to incorporate.

This decision is made individually for each node and each feature dimension.

In practice, this means that the model has more control over how information flows across layers. It can learn to preserve important features from earlier layers while still integrating new signals from the neighborhood. This helps reduce oversmoothing by preventing the full collapse of node representations across the graph.

Such gating mechanisms are used in models like **GRU-GCN**, where a Gated Recurrent Unit is used as the update function for each node (Li et al., 2015; Selsam et al., 2019). These methods introduce more parameters but offer finer control and adaptability, which is especially useful in deeper GNNs.

6.2.4 Jumping Knowledge Networks

In standard GNNs, each node updates its representation layer by layer, and the final output from the last layer is typically used for downstream tasks. This assumes that all nodes benefit equally from aggregating information over the same number of hops. In practice, however, this is rarely true. Some nodes may only need information from immediate neighbors, while others benefit more from deeper aggregation.

Jumping Knowledge (JK) Networks, proposed by Xu et al. (2018), addressed this issue by allowing each node to form its final representation by combining its outputs from multiple GNN layers. Instead of relying only on the final output, the model collects all intermediate representations $h_v^1, h_v^2, \ldots, h_v^L$, one from each layer, and merges them using a differentiable combination function. Formally, the final representation is written as:

$$h_v^{JK} = COMBINE(h_v^l, h_v^2, \ldots, h_v^L)$$

The COMBINE function can be any differentiable function. It may be as simple as concatenation or as flexible as attention-based weighting. For example, using concatenation:

$$h_v^{JK} = [h_v^l \,||\, h_v^2 \,||\, \ldots \,||\, h_v^L]$$

This setup allows the model to select which layer's output is most useful for each node. Nodes that only need shallow information can focus on earlier layers, while others can rely on deeper ones. Because the combination is differentiable, the model can learn these preferences during training. Jumping Knowledge Networks help mitigate oversmoothing by retaining access to features from all layers. They also increase the flexibility of the model without requiring any changes to the base GNN architecture.

Chapter Summary

- GNNs update node features by aggregating messages from neighbors. The way this aggregation and update is performed greatly affects model performance.
- Simple methods like sum and mean treat all neighbors equally, while set pooling introduces learnable functions to extract richer patterns from neighborhoods.
- Neighborhood-based attention learns to assign different weights to different neighbors, allowing the model to focus on more informative nodes.
- As more GNN layers are stacked, nodes receive information from a wider range of the graph. This can lead to oversmoothing, where all node features become nearly identical.
- Oversmoothing can be mitigated by designing smarter update steps:
  - Concatenation preserves earlier features alongside new ones.
  - Skip connections combine new and old features additively.
  - Gated updates allow the model to control how much old and new information to retain.
  - Jumping Knowledge Networks combine outputs from all layers, allowing nodes to adaptively use information from different depths.
- These techniques help build deeper, more expressive, and more robust GNNs for complex graph learning tasks.

Quiz

1. **What property do sum and mean aggregation functions share when used in GNNs?**
   a. Order-sensitivity
   b. Learnability
   c. Permutation invariance
   d. Supervised optimization

2. **Set pooling differs from basic aggregation methods like sum or mean because:**
   a. It does not require node features
   b. It uses a predefined function to transform neighbors
   c. It applies learnable transformations before aggregation
   d. It ignores permutation invariance

3. **Which of the following best describes the role of the MLP in set pooling?**
   a. It normalizes node features
   b. It selects only important neighbors
   c. It transforms each neighbor's features before pooling
   d. It computes the attention weight for each node

4. **The theoretical motivation for set pooling is that:**
   a. It approximates shortest paths
   b. It can model graph connectivity directly
   c. It can approximate any function over sets
   d. It preserves spatial locality

5. **In attention-based aggregation, what does the softmax function do?**
    a. Learns the update rule
    b. Ensures attention weights sum to one
    c. Computes node embeddings
    d. Normalizes edge features

6. **In the original Graph Attention Network (GAT), what activation function is applied before softmax?**
    a. ReLU
    b. Sigmoid
    c. LeakyReLU
    d. Tanh

7. **Which attention scoring mechanism computes attention as $h_v^T W h_u$?**
    a. MLP-based attention
    b. GAT attention
    c. Bilinear attention
    d. Residual attention

8. **What is the primary goal of attention-based aggregation?**
    a. To speed up GNN computation
    b. To compute centrality scores
    c. To weigh neighbor contributions based on importance
    d. To replace node features with random projections

9. **In a GNN with *k* layers, what information does a node have access to?**
   a. Its own past states only
   b. Only its immediate neighbors
   c. All nodes within k-hop neighborhood
   d. Global graph structure

10. **The oversmoothing effect refers to:**
    a. Nodes becoming disconnected over layers
    b. Loss of training signal
    c. Node features becoming indistinguishable across the graph
    d. Overfitting due to too many GNN layers

Answers

1 – c	2 – c	3 – c	4 – c	5 – b
6 – c	7 – c	8 – c	9 – c	10 – c

CHAPTER 7

Applications of Graph Machine Learning

Key Learning Objectives

- Understand how graph machine learning is applied in real-world domains such as social networks, fraud detection, recommender systems, and bioinformatics
- Identify how different types of data (users, transactions, molecules, etc.) can be represented as graphs
- Map real-world problems to appropriate graph learning tasks like node classification, edge prediction, graph classification, and community detection
- Recognize the challenges involved in practical applications, such as class imbalance and cold start
- Access real datasets to explore graph learning tasks hands-on and strengthen your understanding through experimentation

So far, our focus has been on the *how* of the methods and mechanics behind graph machine learning. Now, we shift our attention to *where*. Where are these powerful techniques being used? How do they solve tangible, real-world problems?

This chapter will bring the concepts we've learned to life by exploring several key domains where graph machine learning is making a significant impact. For each application, we will follow a clear and consistent structure. We will first introduce the real-world problem and then define how it can be modeled as a graph, specifying what the nodes and edges represent. We will then identify the specific graph learning task required to solve the problem and, finally, provide a link to a public dataset to encourage hands-on practice.

7.1 Social Network Analysis

One of the most intuitive applications of graph machine learning is in the world of social networks. Think about platforms like Facebook, X (formerly Twitter), or Instagram. At their core, they are massive graphs. Every user on the platform can be thought of as a node, and the connections between them, like friendships, follows, or even likes, form the edges.

By viewing social networks as graphs (as shown in Figure 7.1), we can start to answer some very interesting and complex questions: How does Facebook's "People You May Know" feature work? How can we find the most influential people in a network? And how can we spot fake or automated bot accounts? Let's explore how these questions are addressed using specific graph learning tasks.

Figure 7.1 A social network modeled as a graph

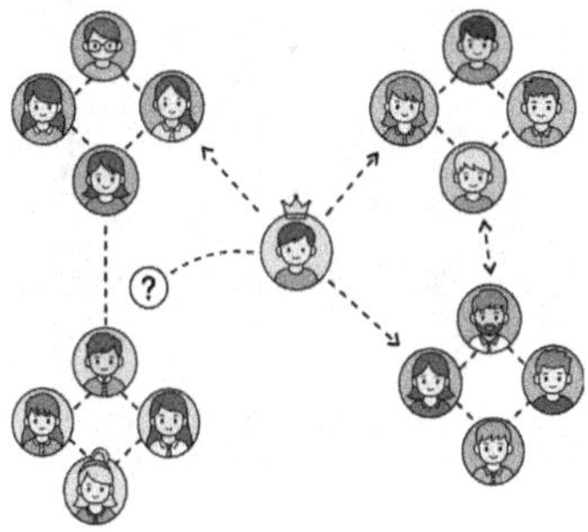

Source: Google Gemini

Prompt: A clean flat vector infographic of a social network modeled as a graph.

Task 1: Understanding and Classifying Users

A fundamental need for social platforms is to understand their users. This could involve predicting a user's interests to recommend relevant content like posts and news articles, or it can be a critical security measure, such as detecting automated bot accounts. Bots often exhibit distinct network patterns, like having thousands of connections with very few mutual friends, that distinguish them from human users. This problem can be solved by framing it as a **node classification** task, where the goal is to assign a label (e.g., an interest like "Sports Fan," or a type like "Bot") to each user node.

Task 2: Recommending New Friends

The "People You May Know" feature is a classic example of predicting future connections. The goal is to identify and suggest potential new friendships by analyzing the network to see which non-existent connections are most likely to form. For instance, if two users share many mutual friends but are not yet connected themselves, they are strong candidates for a recommendation. This task can be solved using **edge prediction** (or link prediction).

Task 3: Identifying Influential Users

In any network, some nodes are more structurally important than others. In social media, identifying these "influencers" is crucial for marketing and for understanding how information and trends spread. The goal is to identify and rank the most critical nodes in the graph based on their position and connectivity. This challenge can be addressed as a **node centrality** or node ranking task.

Dataset for Practice

While we can't use data from platforms like Facebook directly, there are many public social network datasets perfect for practice. One such dataset is the **BlogCatalog social network**.

The Graph Representation

- **Nodes**: Each node represents a blogger.
- **Edges**: An edge connects two bloggers, representing a friendship between them.
- **Features and Labels:** Each blogger has features derived from the keywords in their blog posts. The dataset also includes labels that categorize the bloggers based on their topics of interest. This makes it ideal for practicing **node classification** (predicting interests). You can also use its structure for **edge prediction** (who might become friends) and for analyzing **node centrality** (who are the most influential bloggers).

7.2 Fraud Detection and Cybersecurity

In our increasingly digital world, financial fraud and cyberattacks are persistent threats. Criminals constantly devise sophisticated methods to steal money, compromise accounts, or attack systems. Often, these illicit activities are not isolated events but are part of coordinated efforts involving multiple accounts and entities. This is where graph machine learning becomes an incredibly powerful ally. By modeling financial transactions or network communications as a graph, we can move beyond analyzing individual data points and instead focus on the *relationships* and *patterns* of behavior. This allows us to uncover complex fraud rings and subtle attack patterns that would otherwise go unnoticed.

Task 1: Identifying Fraudulent Transactions or Accounts

Consider a network of cryptocurrency transactions. Most transactions are legitimate ("licit"), but a small fraction are associated with illicit activities like scams, theft, or money laundering. These illicit transactions often leave clues in their connections. For example, they may receive funds from known illicit sources or attempt to obscure their origin through a complex series of tumbling services. The goal is to flag these suspicious transactions before they can be further integrated into the legitimate financial system.

- **The Goal**: To assign a label of "Illicit" or "Licit" to each node (in this case, a transaction) in the graph.
- **Potential solution:** Framing it as a **node classification** task. A GNN can learn the complex features and neighborhood patterns that distinguish illicit transactions from licit ones. For instance, a transaction node connected to other known illicit nodes is more likely to be illicit itself.

Task 2: Detecting Coordinated Illicit Activity

Fraud is often a team sport. Criminals may use a network of accounts and transactions to carry out coordinated illicit activities. In a graph, these entities can form identifiable structures or communities that look different from normal user behavior. For example, a group of transactions might rapidly pass funds through a series of wallets in a circular pattern to launder them. Identifying these groups is a crucial step in dismantling large-scale illicit operations.

- **The Goal**: To identify clusters or subgraphs of nodes that are working together in a coordinated, illicit manner.
- **Potential solution**: Treating it as a **community detection** or **subgraph analysis** task. Graph algorithms can identify these unusually dense and suspiciously interconnected clusters of transactions, flagging the entire ring for investigation.

Figure 7.2 A financial network

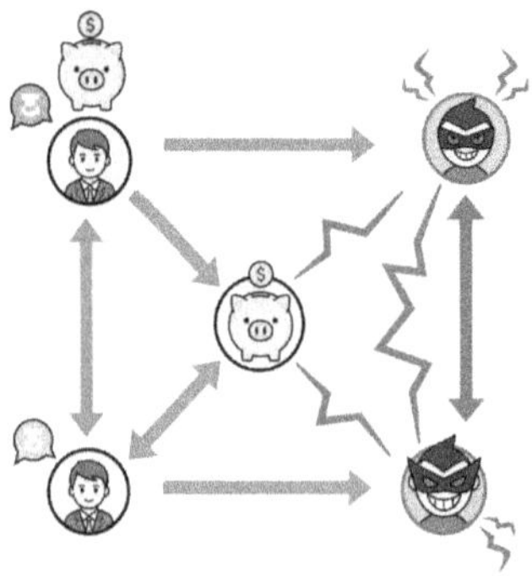

A critical challenge in real-world fraud detection is the extreme class imbalance in the data. In any given dataset, the number of legitimate transactions vastly outnumbers the fraudulent ones, often by a ratio of more than 1000:1. This poses a significant problem for training machine learning models, as the model can achieve high accuracy simply by always predicting "legitimate." To build an effective GNN for fraud detection, special care must be taken to handle this imbalance, for example, by upweighting the loss for the fraudulent class during training or using other specialized sampling techniques to ensure the model learns to identify the rare but critical fraudulent patterns.

Dataset for Practice

A fantastic, graph-native dataset for this type of problem is the **Elliptic Bitcoin Dataset**. It's a real-world transaction graph from the Bitcoin network.

The Graph Representation

- **Nodes**: Each node represents a **Bitcoin transaction**.
- **Edges**: A directed edge represents the flow of Bitcoin from one transaction to another.
- **Features and Labels**: Each transaction node is associated with a time step and 165 anonymized features (e.g., transaction fees, inputs, and outputs). A subset of transactions is labeled as "**illicit**" (associated with scams, malware, etc.) or "**licit**" (associated with exchanges, miners, etc.). This makes it an excellent real-world dataset for practicing node classification for fraud detection.

7.3 Recommender Systems

Have you ever wondered how Netflix knows which movie you'll want to binge next, or how Amazon suggests a product that you suddenly realize you need? The magic behind these features is often powered by recommender systems, and graphs provide a very natural way to build them.

By modeling the entire ecosystem of users and products as a giant network (as shown in Figure 7.3), we can uncover subtle patterns in taste and preference. These systems are often modeled as **bipartite graphs**, graphs with two distinct sets of nodes. In this case, one set of nodes represents the **users**, and the other set represents the **items** (like movies, songs, or products).

Task: Predicting User Preferences

Figure 7.3 **A graph between users and products**

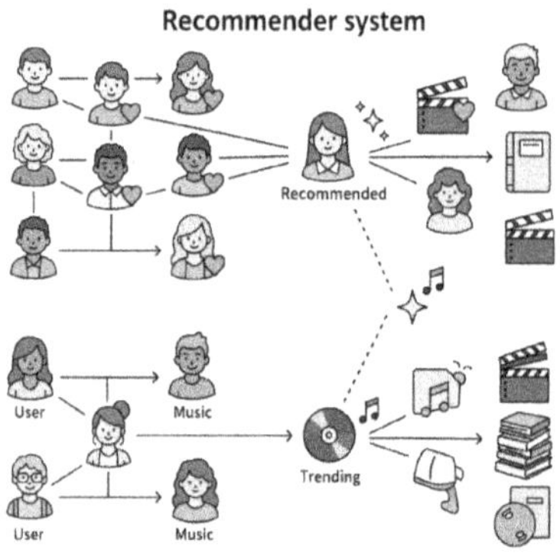

The graph can be used to recommend new products.

Source: Google Gemini

Prompt: A flat vector inforgraphic illustrating a Recommender System flow.

The fundamental goal of a recommender system is to predict what a user will like. In our graph model, an edge exists between a user and an item if the user has interacted with it, for example, by rating a movie or purchasing a product. The core challenge is to figure out which non-existent edges are most likely to be formed in the future. For instance, if you and another user have rated several of the same sci-fi movies highly, and that user has also liked a new sci-fi movie you haven't seen, that movie is a strong candidate for your recommendation list. This task is a classic application of **edge prediction**.

- **The Goal**: To predict the likelihood (or a potential rating score) of a new edge forming between a user node and an item node.
- **Potential solution**: Using edge prediction models. These models learn from the existing network of user-item interactions to identify "missing" links that would represent a successful recommendation.

A major challenge for any recommender system is the **cold start problem**, which arises when there is not enough interaction data to make reliable recommendations. This typically occurs when a new user joins the platform and has no history of purchases or ratings, or when a new item is added and has yet to be discovered by any users. Traditional methods often struggle in these scenarios, but graph-based approaches provide an elegant solution by looking beyond direct user-item interactions.

Graphs have the unique ability to incorporate other sources of information, often called "side information," directly into the network structure. For instance, a new movie can be immediately connected to nodes representing its genre, director, and actors. A GNN can then traverse these connections to recommend this new movie to users who have previously liked other films by the same director or in the same genre. Similarly, if the graph includes a social network component, a new user can be connected to their friends who are already on the platform. The system can then suggest items that this user's friends have enjoyed, using their social circle to provide initial recommendations and overcome the new user cold start. By leveraging this rich, relational context, GNNs can make intelligent and relevant predictions even when direct interaction data is sparse or non-existent.

Dataset for Practice

A classic and widely used dataset for building recommender systems is the **MovieLens dataset**. It's an excellent starting point for anyone interested in this application.

The Graph Representation

- **Nodes**: The graph has two sets of nodes: users and movies.
- **Edges**: An edge exists between a user and a movie if the user has rated that movie. The edge itself can be thought of as having a weight or feature, which is the rating value (e.g., 1 to 5 stars).
- **Features and Labels**: While the primary task uses the graph structure, the dataset also provides metadata like movie genres and timestamps, which can be used as features to enhance the model. The "labels" in this context are the ratings on the edges you are trying to predict.

7.4 Bioinformatics: Drug Discovery and Protein Interaction Networks

Beyond the digital world of social and financial networks, graph machine learning is making a profound impact on biology and medicine. Complex biological systems, from the intricate structure of a molecule to the vast network of interacting proteins in a cell, are naturally represented as graphs. By applying GNNs to these biological graphs, scientists can accelerate drug discovery, understand diseases better, and uncover the fundamental mechanisms of life.

Task 1: Predicting Molecular Properties for Drug Discovery

One of the most expensive and time-consuming parts of creating new medicines is screening millions of potential molecules to see if they might be effective or toxic. Graph

Neural Networks can dramatically speed this up by predicting a molecule's properties directly from its structure.

This is a classic **graph classification** task.

- **The Goal**: To assign a single label to an entire graph (a molecule) to predict its properties, such as its toxicity, solubility, or effectiveness against a particular virus.
- **The Graph Representation**: Each molecule is a graph where nodes are atoms (e.g., Carbon, Oxygen) and edges are the chemical bonds between them.
- **Potential Solution**: Using a graph classification model. The GNN processes the entire molecular graph, its atoms, bonds, and overall structure, to output a single prediction for the molecule as a whole.

Task 2: Analyzing Protein-Protein Interaction (PPI) Networks

Figure 7.4 **Protein-Protein interaction modeled as a graph**

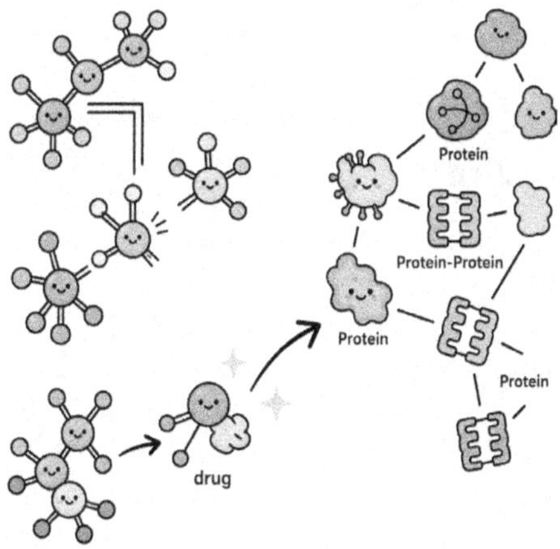

Source: Google Gemini

Prompt: A cute hand-drawn scientific illustration infographic on a white background.

Proteins are the workhorses of our cells, and they rarely act alone. They form complex interaction networks to carry out biological functions. Understanding these interactions is key to understanding diseases, but mapping them out experimentally is difficult. Graph learning can help fill in the gaps by predicting which proteins are likely to interact.

This is an **edge prediction** task.

- **The Goal**: To predict a missing edge between two protein nodes, which would represent a previously unknown biological interaction.
- **The Graph Representation**: In a PPI network (as shown in Figure 7.4), nodes are proteins, and an edge connects two proteins that are known to interact or work together.
- **Potential Solution**: Applying edge prediction models to the PPI network. The model learns from the patterns of known interactions to score and identify new pairs of proteins that are likely to have a functional relationship.

Dataset for Practice

For predicting molecular properties, a well-known benchmark is the **Tox21 dataset**.

The Graph Representation

- **Nodes**: Atoms within a chemical compound.
- **Edges**: Chemical bonds between the atoms.
- **Features and Labels**: The dataset provides the graph structure for thousands of small molecules. Each molecule (graph) is labeled based on its toxicity in 12 different experimental assays. This makes it a perfect dataset for practicing graph classification.

7.5 Optimizing Transportation Networks

Every day, millions of people navigate complex transportation systems, from city streets to global flight paths. These systems are natural graphs, where optimizing flow, predicting traffic, and ensuring resilience are critical tasks. Graph machine learning provides the tools to model and analyze these intricate networks, leading to smarter and more efficient transportation for everyone.

Task: Predicting Traffic Flow

A primary challenge in urban planning is traffic prediction. The goal is to forecast future traffic conditions (e.g., speed or congestion) for different road segments in the network. This is a **graph-level regression** task. In this graph, the nodes represent key locations such as road intersections, airports, or train stations, with features that can capture dynamic sensor data like current traffic volume or the capacity of an airport. The edges are the pathways connecting these locations, like roads, flight routes, or railway tracks, and their features can represent properties such as distance, travel time, or the speed limit.

- **The Goal**: To predict a continuous value (like average speed in km/h) for nodes or edges in the graph at a future point in time.
- **Potential Solution**: Using a GNN that learns from both the graph's structure (how roads are connected) and the dynamic features at each node (real-time traffic sensor data). The model can capture how congestion in one intersection will spread to its neighbors over time.

Dataset for Practice: METR-LA Dataset: This is a famous dataset for traffic forecasting. It contains traffic data from loop detectors in Los Angeles County, including the graph structure of the road network and sensor readings over time.

7.6 Powering Search and Discovery with Knowledge Graphs

Have you ever asked a search engine a complex question like, "Who was the lead actor in the movie directed by the person who also directed *Inception*?" and gotten a direct answer? The technology behind this is often a **Knowledge Graph**. These are massive graphs that store real-world entities and the rich relationships between them, creating a structured web of knowledge.

Task: Completing the Knowledge Graph

Knowledge graphs, despite being massive, are always incomplete. Countless facts and relationships in the world have not been added yet. The goal is to automatically infer and add these missing facts to the graph. In a Knowledge Graph, the nodes represent real-world entities like people (e.g., *Christopher Nolan*), places, events, or even abstract concepts (e.g., *Movie Director*). The edges then represent the rich relationships that connect these entities, and they are often labeled to specify the type of relationship, such as directed_by, acted_in, or born_in.

- **The Goal**: To predict a missing edge (relationship) or a missing node (entity) in a (head_entity, relation, tail_entity) triplet. For example, given (Leonardo DiCaprio, acted_in, ?), the model should predict a movie like *Inception*.

- **Potential Solution**: Treating it as an **edge prediction** (or link prediction) task. Specialized GNNs and embedding models learn vector representations of the entities and relations to predict which connections are plausible, effectively "reasoning" over the graph to fill in the blanks.

It's worth noting that while the link prediction techniques covered in this book provide a strong and intuitive foundation for understanding Knowledge Graph completion, this is a rich and active area of research with its own specialized models. Methods based on tensor factorization or translational embeddings (like the popular TransE family of models) are designed specifically for the unique structure of knowledge graphs and often achieve state-of-the-art performance. The GNN-based approaches we've discussed offer a powerful and generalizable starting point, but we encourage the interested reader to explore these dedicated methods as they continue their learning journey.

Dataset for Practice: Freebase (FB15k-237): Freebase was a large knowledge graph acquired by Google. The FB15k-237 dataset is a standard benchmark derived from it, containing thousands of entities and relationship types, used for the task of knowledge graph completion.

Chapter Summary

- This chapter introduced real-world applications of graph machine learning across various domains, including social networks, fraud detection, recommendation systems, and bioinformatics.
- Each application was explained in terms of what the nodes and edges represent, and how problems are mapped to graph learning tasks like node classification, link prediction, and graph classification.
- We saw how graphs can model user interactions, financial transactions, molecules, transportation systems, and knowledge bases, enabling tasks like fraud detection, traffic forecasting, and drug discovery.
- Real datasets were included for each application to help readers explore the tasks hands-on and build practical understanding.

Quiz

1. **In a social network graph, what does an edge typically represent?**
   a. A user's age
   b. A connection between two users
   c. A community label
   d. An interest score

2. **Which graph learning task is most suitable for predicting fraudulent accounts in a transaction network?**
   a. Edge classification
   b. Node classification
   c. Graph classification
   d. Link prediction

3. **In a recommender system, what does a bipartite graph consist of?**
   a. Users and their feature embeddings
   b. Items connected to other items
   c. Users and items as two disjoint sets of nodes
   d. Products only, with user ratings as features

4. **Predicting whether two proteins interact in a protein–protein interaction network is an example of:**
   a. Edge-level learning
   b. Graph-level learning
   c. Node-level learning
   d. Path prediction

5. **Which of the following is a common challenge in recommender systems modeled as graphs?**
   a. Data overfitting
   b. Cold start problem
   c. Noisy molecular structure
   d. Protein folding error

6. **In molecular property prediction, what do the nodes and edges represent, respectively?**
   a. Atoms and chemical bonds
   b. Genes and enzymes
   c. Reactions and catalysts
   d. Molecules and interactions

7. **Which of these tasks is commonly addressed using knowledge graphs?**
   a. Link prediction
   b. Traffic congestion estimation
   c. Graph classification
   d. Community detection

8. **A traffic sensor network is best modeled as what kind of graph?**
   a. Temporal multigraph
   b. Directed sensor graph
   c. Spatial-temporal graph
   d. Bipartite user-item graph

9. **Community detection in social networks typically falls under:**
   a. Supervised graph classification
   b. Unsupervised node-level learning
   c. Reinforcement learning
   d. Graph embedding

10. **What kind of graph task is "recommending a new connection between users" in a social network?**
    a. Community prediction
    b. Node classification
    c. Link prediction
    d. Graph-level prediction

Answers

1 – b	2 – b	3 – c	4 – a	5 – b
6 – a	7 – a	8 – c	9 – b	10 – c

CHAPTER 8

Practical Considerations in Graph ML

Key Learning Objectives

- Understand how to construct a graph from raw tabular or relational data
- Explain why full-batch training is inefficient for large graphs and how techniques like neighbor sampling, layer-wise sampling, and subgraph sampling help overcome this
- Identify the difference between over-squashing and oversmoothing, and how each affects model performance
- Choose an appropriate number of GNN layers depending on the task and graph structure

Throughout this book, we have built a strong foundation in the world of Graph Machine Learning. We began with the basic question of what a graph is, journeyed through the mechanics of how Graph Neural Networks learn by passing messages, and explored a diverse landscape of their real-world applications. We have covered the theory and seen the potential.

However, there is often a gap between understanding a model in a clean, academic setting and applying it to a messy, real-world problem. This chapter is designed to bridge that gap. It addresses the practical questions and challenges that inevitably arise when you move from a textbook example to your own project.

Think of the journey so far as learning the rules of a complex and powerful game. Now, we step onto the field to play. We will discuss how to handle the sheer scale of real-world graphs, what to do when your data doesn't look like a graph to begin with, and how to navigate the subtle but critical pitfalls in model design and evaluation that can mean the difference between success and failure. This chapter will equip you with the practical wisdom needed to not only understand GNNs but also to use them effectively.

8.1 Graph Construction: From Data to Graph

One of the most common situations when starting a graph machine learning project is this: you have data, but it's not in the form of a graph. You might have a table of users and their attributes, a list of transactions, or rows in a spreadsheet, and no obvious nodes and edges. In such cases, the first step is to **construct a graph** from the available data in a way that is meaningful and useful for learning.

Graphs from tabular data can be constructed depending on what the data represents. The idea behind graph construction is to decide what your nodes and edges will be. In most cases, one data point in tabular data becomes a node, and then one defines the rules that create edges, or connections, between them. Sometimes, this rule for creating edges between nodes is explicit, like friendships in a social network or citations between papers. But often, the connections need to be created based on similarity, interaction, or some form of shared behavior between nodes. This is less a rigid procedure and more a creative modeling exercise, where the best design depends on the problem you want to solve.

For example, if you're working with user data of an e-commerce website, each user could be a node. You might connect users with an edge if they have purchased the same items, visited similar product pages, or rated similar things. In a financial dataset, each node might represent an account, and edges could be created between accounts that appear in the same transaction chains.

Another approach is to create graphs using k-nearest neighbors (k-NN), using a suitable distance metric in the feature space. For example, when working with tabular data with numerical features, you can compute the similarity between every pair of samples. Edges can be added from each node to its k most similar neighbors. This is a common approach in bioinformatics and recommendation systems.

Another way to create a graph is to use domain knowledge to define edges. For example, in chemistry, the structure of a molecule (which atoms are connected by which bonds) is already known. These bonds can be directly used as edges to create the graph.

The key idea in all these methods is that the way you build the graph should reflect the kind of relationship that matters for the task you're solving. There is no correct or incorrect way to construct a graph; it depends entirely on your data and the task at hand. Once you have created the graph, you can proceed with defining features for the nodes (and possibly the edges) and choosing a graph learning task, such as node classification or link prediction.

Graph construction is not a one-time decision. It often takes several iterations to find a structure that works well. The goal is to capture useful relationships in the graph while avoiding noise or spurious connections that may mislead the learning process.

In short, even if your data does not initially look like a graph, chances are high that it can be turned into one with the right strategy. And once you have a graph that represents your data well, you unlock the full power of GNNs to model complex relationships and improve performance.

8.2 Scalability: Training GNNs on Large Graphs

The GNN architectures we have discussed in this book are powerful and effective, but they are designed for full-batch training. This means that at every layer, the GNN model computes the embeddings for every node in the graph at once. In this process, the model needs to have the entire graph structure (the adjacency matrix) and all of the node features loaded into memory. This makes scaling expensive when we move from academic datasets to real-world graphs. To do this, the model needs to have the entire graph structure (the adjacency matrix) and all of the node features loaded into memory. This is simply impossible for graphs with millions or even billions of nodes. The memory requirements would be enormous, and the computation for even a single forward pass would be prohibitively slow. The solution is to borrow a familiar concept from traditional deep learning, known as mini-batch training. Instead of processing the whole graph at once, we process a small batch of nodes at a time. However, we can't just pick random nodes and treat them as independent data points. The very nature of a GNN is that a node's representation depends on its neighbors, which in turn depend on their neighbors. This creates a complex web of dependencies. If we select a mini-batch of nodes to update, we quickly realize we need information from a much larger portion of the graph.

This challenge is solved by a clever and highly effective technique known as **neighbor sampling**, popularized by the **GraphSAGE** model (Hamilton et al., 2017).

Neighbor Sampling

Instead of trying to compute embeddings for all nodes, neighbor sampling works backward from a small batch of target nodes (the ones we'll use to calculate our loss for that step). It builds a small, localized "computation graph" for just that batch.

Let's walk through how it works for a 2-layer GNN:

Step 0: Select Target Nodes

We start by selecting a mini-batch of nodes whose final embeddings we want to compute. Let's call this Batch_0.

Step 1: Sample Neighbors for the Final Layer (Layer 2)

To compute the Layer 2 embeddings for the nodes in Batch_0, each node needs to aggregate messages from its neighbors. Instead of using *all* neighbors, each node in Batch_0 randomly samples a fixed number of its neighbors. For example, we might decide to sample just 10 neighbors for each node, regardless of whether a node has 50 or 5000 actual neighbors. Let's call the set of these sampled neighbors Batch_1.

Step 2: Sample Neighbors for the First Layer (Layer 1)

Now, to compute the Layer 1 embeddings for the nodes in Batch_1 (which are needed for the next step), we repeat the process. Each node in Batch_1 randomly samples a fixed number of its own neighbors. Let's call this final set of nodes Batch_2.

The Forward Pass: From the Bottom Up.

Now that we have our small computation graph, the forward pass happens in reverse.

- First, we take the input features of the nodes in Batch_2.
- Using these features, we compute the Layer 1 embeddings for the nodes in Batch_1. Each node in Batch_1 aggregates messages *only* from its sampled neighbors in Batch_2.
- Finally, using the new Layer 1 embeddings for Batch_1, we compute the final Layer 2 embeddings for our target nodes in Batch_0. Each node in Batch_0 aggregates messages *only* from its sampled neighbors in Batch_1.

By doing this, we have successfully computed the final embeddings for our target mini-batch without ever looking at the entire graph. The amount of computation for each node is now constant, which is determined by the number of samples we take, and not by the node's true degree. This makes the process incredibly efficient and allows GNNs to scale to massive graphs. While we are introducing an approximation by not using all neighbors, this technique has proven to be highly effective in practice.

Layer-wise Sampling

FastGCN (Chen et al., 2018) proposes a different strategy called **layer-wise sampling**. Instead of sampling neighbors for each node, FastGCN samples a fixed number of nodes for each GNN layer from a global distribution. This avoids the exponential blow-up in neighborhood size that occurs with node-wise sampling.

However, this approach may suffer from a mismatch between sampled nodes and the actual local structure around the nodes in the mini-batch.

Cluster-based and Graph Partitioning Methods

Cluster-GCN (Chiang et al., 2019) takes a different route. It preprocesses the graph into **clusters** using algorithms like METIS. Each cluster is treated as a mini-batch during training. Since all nodes within a cluster are densely connected, this strategy reduces message-passing across batches and improves memory locality.

Cluster-based methods avoid neighbor sampling altogether and are often more efficient when the graph is static. However, the quality of the clustering impacts performance and must be chosen carefully.

Subgraph Sampling

Another popular approach is subgraph sampling, used in models like **GraphSAINT** (Zeng et al., 2020). Instead of sampling nodes or neighbors, GraphSAINT samples random subgraphs of the full graph and applies standard GCN operations within each subgraph.

This technique combines the benefits of sampling and full-batch aggregation, achieving high accuracy while maintaining scalability.

Other Strategies

Some additional strategies for handling large graphs include:

- Caching frequently used node embeddings to avoid recomputation (Zheng et al., 2020).
- Using simple aggregators like mean or sum to reduce computational cost.
- Adopting distributed training, where the graph is partitioned and spread across machines or GPUs. This is supported in libraries like **DGL** (Wang et al., 2019) and **PyG**.

8.3 Over-squashing: The Information Bottleneck

When a Graph Neural Network underperforms, a common suspect is the **oversmoothing** problem we discussed earlier, which occurs when stacking too many layers. However, there is another, more subtle issue that can plague GNNs even with a shallow architecture: **over-squashing**. While the two are related, they are not the same. Oversmoothing is a problem of *depth*, where node embeddings become too similar. Over-squashing is a problem of *structure*, where the graph has "bottlenecks" that compress, or "squash," information as it flows through the network (as shown in Figure 8.1).

To build an intuition, imagine a GNN is trying to pass a message from a node on one side of a large graph to a node on the other side. If that message must pass through a single, central node (a bottleneck), that central node's fixed-size embedding vector has to act as a channel for all the information from one half of the graph to the other. It's like trying to fit the contents of an entire library onto a single postcard. Important details are inevitably lost.

Figure 8.1 Example of a graph in which we observe over-squashing

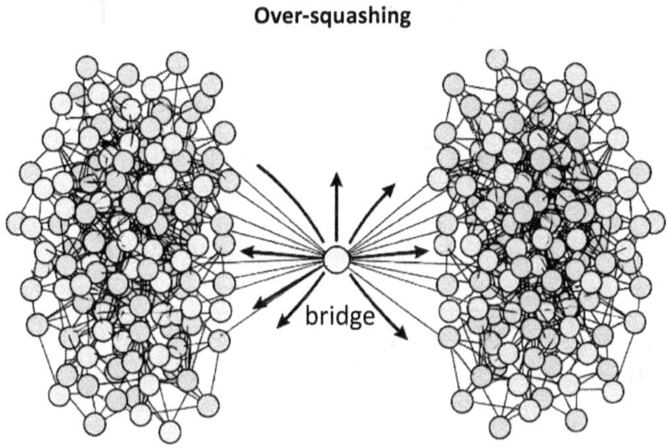

Source: Google Gemini

Prompt: A scientific diagram titled "over-squashing" on a white background.

Two large, dense clusters of green and blue nodes are connected to a single, small central "bridge" node by many converging arrows, illustrating an information bottleneck.

Why Does Over-squashing Happen?

The root of the problem lies in the exponential growth of a node's receptive field. In many graphs, especially those that are tree-like, the number of nodes in a *k*-hop neighborhood grows exponentially with *k*. A standard GNN layer, however, compresses all the information from this large neighborhood into a single, fixed-size vector for the central node.

This compression becomes a major issue when the model needs to learn long-range dependencies. For a node v to be influenced by a distant node u, the gradient of the loss function with respect to v must be successfully backpropagated all the way to u. However, when information is "squashed" at a bottleneck node during the forward pass, the gradients flowing backward through that same bottleneck can vanish or become highly distorted. The model effectively becomes "blind" to the influence of distant nodes because the message-passing path is too narrow.

This is particularly problematic in graphs with:

- **High Curvature or Tree-like Structures**: Where neighborhoods expand very rapidly.
- **"Bridge" Edges**: A single edge or a small set of edges that connect two dense communities. Any information passing between these communities is forced through this narrow bridge and is highly susceptible to being squashed.

Many real-world graphs in domains like drug discovery and social network analysis exhibit these properties, making over-squashing a critical practical concern.

Techniques to Mitigate Over-squashing

While there is no single perfect solution, several strategies have been developed to alleviate the information bottleneck:

- **Graph Rewiring**: The most direct approach is to alter the graph's structure to create better information flow. This involves adding new edges, or "shortcuts," that bypass the bottlenecks. For example, one could add edges between all nodes that are 2 hops away from each other. More advanced methods use metrics like graph curvature to identify bottlenecks and strategically add edges to relieve the pressure.
- **Richer Message Passing**: Instead of compressing all neighborhood information into a single vector, some advanced GNN architectures allow for more expressive messages. This might involve passing sets of node embeddings or using attention mechanisms that can

learn to dynamically focus on the most important information, preventing it from being drowned out.

- **Increasing Node Capacity**: Since the node embedding is the bottleneck, another solution is to increase its capacity. This could be as simple as using a larger embedding dimension for all nodes, or more sophisticated, by adaptively increasing the dimension only for nodes that are identified as potential bottlenecks.

In practice, diagnosing model performance issues requires thinking about both the depth of your model (oversmoothing) and the structure of your graph (over-squashing). If your task requires learning long-range dependencies and your GNN is failing, investigating your graph for bottlenecks is a crucial next step.

8.4 Choosing Model Depth and the Oversmoothing Problem

A common and critical question that arises when designing a GNN architecture is, "How many layers should I use?" In traditional deep learning, the answer is often "the deeper, the better," but GNNs behave differently. As we have briefly discussed before, the main culprit is the **oversmoothing problem**.

When you stack too many GNN layers, the iterative process of neighborhood aggregation causes the embeddings of all nodes in the graph to converge toward a single, uniform value. After a certain number of layers, the individual features of each node are washed out, making them indistinguishable from one another. This severely hurts the model's performance, as it loses the ability to differentiate between nodes for any downstream task.

The practical advice for this is straightforward:

Start shallow

For most applications and standard GNN architectures, you should begin with a shallow model, typically just **2 to 3 layers**. This is often enough to capture meaningful neighborhood information without falling victim to oversmoothing.

Refer to advanced solutions when needed

If your specific application requires capturing information from a larger neighborhood (more "hops" away), a deep, plain GNN is not the answer. Instead, you should implement the more robust architectures discussed in **Chapter 6**, such as adding **skip connections** or using **Jumping Knowledge (JK) Networks**, which are specifically designed to mitigate the oversmoothing effect and allow for deeper models.

Chapter Summary

- Many real-world datasets are not graphs by default. This chapter introduced practical strategies for constructing graphs from raw data using similarity, interaction, or domain knowledge.
- Standard GNN training doesn't scale well to large graphs. We explored scalable alternatives like neighbor sampling (GraphSAGE), layer-wise sampling (FastGCN), cluster-based batching (Cluster-GCN), and subgraph sampling (GraphSAINT).
- We examined the concept of over-squashing, where structural bottlenecks in the graph cause distant signals to be compressed and lost, and discussed solutions like graph rewiring and attention-based aggregation.
- We revisited the oversmoothing problem, which makes node embeddings indistinguishable in deep GNNs, and discussed how shallow architectures or enhanced designs like skip connections and Jumping Knowledge networks can help.

Quiz

1. **What is the main goal of graph construction when starting with tabular data?**
   a. Creating sparse node embeddings
   b. Finding edge weights from training loss
   c. Converting raw data into a meaningful graph structure
   d. Binarizing categorical features

2. **What typically happens during oversmoothing in GNNs?**
   a. Gradients vanish in the early layers
   b. Node embeddings become nearly identical
   c. Edges are deleted during training
   d. Feature dimensions collapse to zero

3. **Over-squashing is caused primarily by:**
   a. Too many parameters in GNNs
   b. Model underfitting due to small graphs
   c. Bottlenecks in graph structure restricting message flow
   d. Data leakage across the test set

4. **4. In GraphSAGE, scalability is achieved by:**
   a. Computing the Laplacian matrix
   b. Sampling a fixed number of neighbors
   c. Training only on leaf nodes
   d. Using edge dropout

5. **What is a good reason to use skip connections in GNNs?**
   a. To reduce the number of training epochs
   b. To avoid memory fragmentation
   c. To preserve earlier layer features and reduce oversmoothing
   d. To boost training loss quickly

6. **A graph with very few edge-disjoint paths between regions is likely to suffer from:**
   a. Overfitting
   b. Oversmoothing
   c. Over-squashing
   d. Under-sampling

7. **In graph construction, how can we define edges if explicit links are missing?**
   a. Random walk frequency
   b. Using node ranking
   c. Based on similarity or shared behavior
   d. Optimizing edge loss

8. **What is one downside of neighborhood sampling in GraphSAGE?**
   a. It completely removes connections
   b. It leads to fixed graph layouts
   c. It introduces stochasticity in training
   d. It increases parameter count exponentially

9. **What is a common approach to reducing over-squashing?**
   a. Adding more attention heads
   b. Rewiring the graph to reduce bottlenecks
   c. Dropping half the edges
   d. Using a shallower network

10. **In which type of graph structure is over-squashing most likely to occur?**
    a. Complete graphs
    b. Highly clustered graphs
    c. Tree-like or chain graphs
    d. Directed cyclic graphs

Answers

1 – c	2 – b	3 – c	4 – b	5 – c
6 – c	7 – c	8 – c	9 – b	10 – c

APPENDIX A:

A Brief Recap Of Machine Learning

Let's begin with something simple: imagine you are given the following pairs of values:

x	1	2	3	4
$f(x)$	5	7	9	11

You might quickly notice a pattern. If someone asks you to guess the value of $f(10)$, chances are, you would respond with **23**. Why?

Because the outputs seem to follow a clear rule:

$$f(x)=2x+3$$

This is an example of a task where you were not given the function explicitly, but you were able to observe a pattern in the data and use it to make a prediction. You didn't memorize all possible values of $f(x)$, instead, you inferred the rule that connects inputs to outputs. This is the basic idea behind machine learning. Machine learning is about finding patterns in data. Specifically, it is about learning a function $f(x)$ from data points, such that it can be used to predict outputs for new, unseen inputs.

A.1 Linear Regression:

Suppose you're given the following data points (as in Figure A.1):

Figure A.1 Real-world data sampled from a line

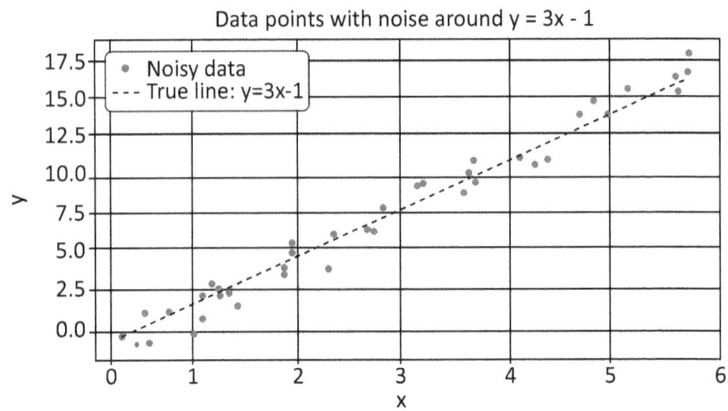

You might notice that these points no longer lie exactly on a perfect line. However, they do appear to roughly follow a trend. They would fall close to a straight line, perhaps something like: **y ≈ 3x - 1**

But the values don't match the rule perfectly. That's because real-world data often contains noise, small errors, inconsistencies, or variations that make it imperfect. The function you're trying to learn is still there, but it's now hidden beneath the noise.

So, how do we handle this? We don't try to find a rule that fits the points exactly; instead, we try to find the line that best fits the data. But what do we mean by *best*? Here's the key idea: the best-fitting line is the one that has the smallest total error between the predicted outputs (what the line says) and the actual outputs (what the data says). This idea leads us to one of the most fundamental problems in machine learning: Find the function f(x) such that the error between f(x) and the actual y values is as small as possible. This task is called **linear regression**, and it's one of the simplest and most widely used techniques in machine learning.

To make this idea more precise, suppose you're given a set of *n* data points $(x_1, y_1), (x_2, y_2), \ldots, (x_n, y_n)$. We want to find a function $f^*(x) = wx + b$, a simple line, that gives predictions $y_i^* = f^*(x_i)$ as close as possible to the actual values Y_i. To measure how far off our predictions are, we use a **loss function**. One of the most common choices is the **squared error**: Loss at point $i = (y_i - y_i^*)^2$. To get the overall error across all points, we sum these individual losses:

$$Total\ Loss = L = \sum_{i=1}^{n} (y_i - f^*(x_i))^2 = \sum_{i=1}^{n} (y_i - (w \times x_i + b))^2$$

This total loss is what we try to **minimize**. The values of w and b that give the smallest loss define the best-fitting line.

Generalizing to Multiple Features:

In our last example, we worked with a single variable, a function like $(x) = 3x - 1$, where x is just one number. But in real-life scenarios, outcomes often depend on multiple factors. Let's take a concrete example. Suppose you're trying to predict the price of a house. The price doesn't depend only on the size of the house, but also on other factors like: the number of bedrooms, distance from the city, age of the building, local school ratings, crime rate, etc. We can represent these features as a set of variables $x_1, x_2, x_3, \ldots, x_n$. Our goal is to **learn a function** that takes these variables as input and gives us the predicted price:

$$y = f(x_1, x_2, x_3, \ldots, x_n)$$

Just like before, we don't know the exact form of this function, but we do have examples of inputs (house features) and outputs (prices). So, just as we did with the noisy line, we try to **find a function** f' that gives predictions close to the true values by minimizing the total loss across the dataset. This idea, learning an approximate function from data by reducing the error, lies at the heart of machine learning.

Minimizing the Error Using Gradient Descent

When we try to fit a model to real-world data, our goal is to find values of the parameters that make the model's predictions as close as possible to the actual outputs. We've seen that this means choosing weights and a bias such that the **total error**, often measured as the sum of squared differences between predicted and actual values, is as small as possible.

In many cases, especially when the model has several inputs or is part of a more complex pipeline, we rely on a method called **gradient descent**. This is an iterative technique that helps us adjust the parameters little by little in a direction that reduces the error. The key idea comes from calculus. The gradient of a function tells us the direction in which it increases the fastest. So, if we want to reduce a function, the most effective direction to move in is opposite to the gradient. That's exactly what gradient descent does. Each parameter is moved in the direction that reduces the loss the most, but how much to move in the negative gradient direction. The size of each step is controlled by a small positive constant (hyperparameter) called the **step length**, often referred to as the *learning rate*, and denoted by θ. For a model with multiple inputs:

$$f(x_1, x_2, \ldots, x_n) = w_1 x_1 + w_2 x_2 + \ldots + w_n x_n + b$$

The weights and biases are updated as follows:

$$w_j := w_j - \theta . \frac{\partial L}{\partial w_j}, and\ b := b - \theta . \frac{\partial L}{\partial b}$$

Here, $\frac{\partial L}{\partial w_j}$ and $\frac{\partial L}{\partial b}$ tell us how much the loss would change if we slightly increased or decreased each parameter. The step length θ controls how far we actually move in that direction. These updates are repeated many times. With each pass over the data, the parameters move closer to values that minimize the error. The process continues until the changes become very small or the loss stops decreasing, which means the model has learned as well as it can from the data. For more details on the gradient descent method, please refer to Section 12.3 of Zhang et. al.

Nonlinear Feature Augmentation

So far, we have used linear models where the prediction was a weighted combination of the input features. This works well when the underlying relationship between inputs and outputs is linear. However, many real-world patterns are more complex and cannot be captured using just straight lines. For example, the output might depend on x^2, or some combination like $x_1 \cdot x_2$, or even a more complex expression such as *sin (x)*. In such cases, no matter how much we fine-tune the weights of a plain linear model, it will never truly fit the data well.

Fortunately, we don't have to abandon linear models entirely. A powerful trick is to transform the input features before feeding them into the model. This approach is known as **nonlinear feature augmentation**. The idea is simple: we keep the model linear in the parameters, but we change the input representation so that the model becomes capable of capturing nonlinear relationships. For instance, if we have a single input variable xxx, and we suspect the target output depends on x^2, we can define a new model like:

$$f(x) = w_1 + w_2\, x^2 + b$$

Even though the function is nonlinear in x, it remains linear in w_1 and w_2, which means we can train it just like any other linear model using gradient descent. This gives us the flexibility to learn curves and more complex shapes, without changing the core training procedure.

The same idea extends to higher dimensions. Suppose we have two input features x_1 and x_2, and we believe their interaction matters. Then we can include terms like $x_1^2, x_2^2, x_1 . x_2$ in the input. Our model might look like:

$$f(x_1, x_2) = w_1 x_1 w_2 x_2 + w_3 x_1^2 + w_4 x_2^2 + w_5 x_1 . x_2 + b$$

This is still a linear model with respect to the weights, but it's now capable of capturing rich and flexible patterns in the data. By choosing the right features, we can make linear regression behave like a powerful nonlinear learner, all without changing its mathematical foundation.

Before moving on, it's worth noting that there are many choices we make while building a machine learning model. We can use different kinds of **loss functions** depending on the problem; for instance, squared error is common for regression, but others like absolute error or Huber loss are also used in certain situations. Some values, like the learning rate or the degree of feature augmentation, are not learned directly from the data; instead, we set them manually. These are known as **hyperparameters**. Deciding how many and what kind of features to include is also important; adding too many can make the model overfit the training data, while too few can cause underfitting. To help control this trade-off, techniques like **regularization** are often used. For a more detailed discussion on these ideas please refer to Chapter 4 ('Training Models') of *Hands-On Machine Learning with Scikit-Learn, Keras, and TensorFlow* by Aurélien Géron. We have also included some good resources in the reference section.

A.2 Introduction to Classification

Up to this point, we have focused on problems where the target output was a continuous number, such as predicting the price of a house or estimating the value of a function. This type of task is called **regression**. The goal there was to learn a function $f(x)$ that maps input features to real numbers while minimizing a loss that reflects the distance between predictions and true values.

But in many real-world problems, the output is not a number; it is a category or label. For example, based on a patient's symptoms and test results, we may want to predict whether they have a particular disease (yes or no). Or, given an image, we may want to identify whether it shows a cat, a dog, or a car. These are examples of classification problems.

At first glance, classification might seem very different from regression, but the underlying learning framework remains quite similar. We still have a dataset of inputs and corresponding outputs, and we still aim to learn a function that can predict outputs for new inputs. The key difference lies in the type of output: instead of predicting a real number, we now want to predict a **class label**, often represented by values like 0 or 1 in the simplest case.

The change in the output space means that we need to modify the way we define our prediction function and the way we measure its error. A linear model like $f(x)=z=w_1 x_1+w_2 x_2+b$ will still form the core of our approach, but we can't use it directly to produce a class label; we need to turn this output into something that represents a probability, typically between 0 and 1, which can then be interpreted as the likelihood of belonging to a particular class. This brings us naturally to the next idea: logistic regression, which is one of the simplest and most widely used methods for binary classification. It builds directly on the ideas of linear regression, with just a small yet powerful twist.

Instead of using this value z directly as our prediction, we now pass it through a special function called the **sigmoid** (also known as the logistic function), defined as:

$$\sigma(z)=\frac{1}{1+e^{-z}}$$

This function has a smooth S-shaped curve and always produces a value between 0 and 1. For very large positive z, the output approaches 1. For very negative z, the output approaches 0. Values near 0 give results close to 0.5. This makes the sigmoid function ideal for modeling probabilities; it tells us how likely the input belongs to the positive class (usually labeled as 1).

So in logistic regression, the prediction for an input $f(x)$ becomes:

$$y^{*}=\sigma(w_1\, x_1+w_2\, x_2+b)$$

This y* is interpreted as the probability that the input belongs to class 1. If it's greater than 0.5, we may predict class 1; otherwise, class 0. (The threshold can be changed depending on the application.)

Just like in regression, we now need a loss function to train this model. But we no longer want to minimize squared error. For classification, a more appropriate loss is the **cross-entropy loss**, which is designed to measure the distance between predicted probabilities and actual class labels (0 or 1). The cross-entropy loss for one data point is:

$$L=-y\, log(y^{*})-(1-y)\, log(1-y^{*})$$

Like before, we can use gradient descent to minimize this loss across the training data. Thus, logistic regression gives us a simple, elegant way to perform binary classification using the same machinery we developed for regression, with just a few key modifications, interpreting outputs as probabilities and using a different loss function. It's often the first method tried in real-world classification tasks, and a powerful building block for more complex models.

A.3 The Perceptron: A Different View of Linear Classification

Logistic regression approaches classification by predicting probabilities and then interpreting them using a threshold (like 0.5) to assign class labels. The perceptron, one of the earliest models in machine learning, takes a more direct approach: it predicts class labels without using probabilities.

The core idea of the perceptron is actually quite similar to what we've already seen. It starts with a linear combination of the input features:

$$z = w_1 x_1 + w_2 x_2 + \ldots + w_n x_n + b$$

But instead of passing this value through a sigmoid function to get a probability, the perceptron uses a **step function**:

$$y^* = \begin{cases} 1, & z \geq 0 \\ 0, & z < 0 \end{cases}$$

In other words, the perceptron draws a straight line (or a hyperplane in higher dimensions) and decides class membership based on which side of that line the input lies.

Just like logistic regression, the perceptron is a **linear classifier**. The key difference is that logistic regression is probabilistic and smooth; it gives soft outputs and can be trained using gradient descent on a smooth loss (cross-entropy). The perceptron, on the other hand, makes hard decisions and is trained using a different update rule that doesn't rely on differentiable loss functions.

The perceptron update rule works like this: for each training point, if the prediction is wrong, the weights are nudged in the direction that would correct the mistake. Mathematically, if the model predicts 0 but the correct label is 1, it adds the input vector to the weights. If the model predicts 1 but the label is 0, it subtracts the input vector. This simple rule gradually adjusts the weights to reduce mistakes.

Although logistic regression and the perceptron start from the same base, a weighted sum of inputs, they differ in how they handle outputs and learning. The perceptron is faster and simpler, but logistic regression is more flexible and reliable, especially when the data is not perfectly separable.

In practice, logistic regression is more commonly used because of its probabilistic interpretation and smoother optimization. However, the perceptron remains historically important and introduces the idea that we can build even more powerful models by stacking and chaining such simple units together, which leads us to **neural networks**.

A.4 Multilayer Perceptrons: Learning Nonlinear Functions

So far, both logistic regression and the perceptron model make predictions using **linear functions** of the input. That means the decision boundaries they learn, the line or surface that separates different classes, are straight. But what if the data cannot be separated by a straight line?

Imagine trying to classify points that lie in concentric circles or spirals. No matter how you adjust the weights of a linear model, it will never be able to draw a curved boundary to separate them correctly. To handle such cases, we need models that can learn **nonlinear functions**.

This is where **Multilayer Perceptrons (MLPs)** come in. An MLP is a network of multiple perceptron-like units arranged in layers. It typically consists of:

- An input layer that receives the feature vector.
- One or more hidden layers, where each node (called a neuron) computes a weighted sum of its inputs and applies a **nonlinear activation function.**
- An output layer that produces the final prediction, for example, a probability via a sigmoid function for binary classification.

A simple MLP with **two hidden layers** works like this:

1. **First hidden layer:** each neuron computes a nonlinear transformation of the input features:

$$h_j^1 = \sigma\left(w_{j1}^{(1)}x_1 + w_{j2}^{(1)}x_2 + \ldots + w_{jn}^{(1)}x_n + b_j^{(1)}\right)$$

2. **Second hidden layer:** neurons operate on the outputs of the first hidden layer:

$$h_j^2 = \sigma\left(w_{j1}^{(2)}h_1^1 + w_{j2}^{(2)}h_2^1 + \ldots + w_{jn}^{(2)}h_m^1 + b_j^{(2)}\right)$$

3. **Output layer:** produces the final prediction using the second hidden layer's outputs:

$$y^* = \sigma\left(v_1h_1^2 + v_2h_2^2 + \ldots + v_rh_m^2 + c\right)$$

As before, σ is an activation function like ReLU, sigmoid, or tanh, applied element-wise. By adding more layers and nonlinear activations, MLPs can model complex, nonlinear patterns that linear models simply cannot capture. By stacking layers and applying nonlinear activations, MLPs can represent complex decision boundaries and capture patterns that linear models cannot. The nonlinearity is crucial; without it, even multiple layers would collapse into a single linear transformation.

MLPs are trained using a method called backpropagation, which uses gradient descent to adjust weights layer by layer, based on how much each contributes to the final error. With enough neurons and layers, MLPs can approximate virtually any function, a fact known as the **universal approximation theorem**. This makes them extremely powerful, and they form the foundation of modern deep learning.

While MLPs may seem like a small step from logistic regression, they mark the beginning of a major leap in capability, allowing us to learn rich, nonlinear relationships in data, whether for regression, classification, or more complex tasks.

The goal of Appendix A has been to refresh the reader's memory and provide a simple, intuitive walkthrough of the foundational ideas in machine learning. From regression to classification and neural networks, the focus has been on building a basic mental model that will help in understanding graph-based learning methods. For a more detailed and rigorous treatment of these topics, including advanced techniques, theoretical underpinnings, and practical implementations, readers are encouraged to refer to dedicated textbooks and online courses on machine learning.

APPENDIX B:

Introduction to PyTorch Geometric (PyG)

PyTorch Geometric (PyG) is a powerful and popular open-source library for writing and training Graph Neural Networks (GNNs) and other deep learning methods on graph-structured data. It is built upon PyTorch and provides a high-level, user-friendly API for handling graph data, implementing GNN layers, and building complete learning pipelines. Its seamless integration with PyTorch, extensive collection of state-of-the-art models and datasets, and excellent performance make it an essential tool for any researcher or practitioner in the field of graph machine learning.

This appendix provides a practical introduction to the core functionalities of PyG. We will walk through the fundamental steps of creating graphs, performing basic operations, loading standard datasets, defining a GNN model, and training it for a node classification task.

B.1 Installation

Before we can use PyG, we need to install it along with its dependencies. PyG's installation depends on your specific system configuration, including your operating system,

CUDA version (if you have a compatible NVIDIA GPU), and the version of PyTorch you have installed.

B.1.1 Checking your CUDA Version (for GPU users)

If you have an NVIDIA GPU and plan to use it for training, you first need to know which version of the CUDA toolkit is compatible with your drivers. You can check this by running the following command in your terminal or command prompt:

```
nvidia-smi
```

This command will output a table of information about your GPU. The CUDA version is typically listed in the top right corner. This is the maximum version of CUDA your driver supports, and you can install any PyTorch version compatible with this CUDA version or lower.

B.1.2 Installing PyTorch and PyG

The recommended way to install PyG is to use the official installation helper on the PyG website, which generates the correct pip command for your setup.

First, ensure you have PyTorch installed. If not, you can install it using a command like the following (please refer to the official PyTorch website for the command best suited for your system). The backslash (\) is used to split a single command across multiple lines for readability.

```
# Example for a system with CUDA 11.8
pip install torch torchvision torchaudio \
  --index-url https://download.pytorch.org/whl/cu118
```

Once PyTorch is installed, you can install the core PyG packages. The exact command will depend on your PyTorch version and CUDA version. A common command looks like this:

```
pip install torch_geometric
pip install torch_sparse torch_scatter \
  torch_cluster torch_spline_conv \
  -f https://data.pyg.org/whl/torch-
${TORCH}+${CUDA}.html
```

You would replace `${TORCH}` with your PyTorch version (e.g., 2.1.0) and `${CUDA}` with your CUDA version (e.g., `cu118` or `cpu` if you don't have a GPU). For example, for PyTorch 2.1.0 and CUDA 11.8, the command would be:

```
pip install torch_sparse torch_scatter \
  torch_cluster torch_spline_conv \
  -f https://data.pyg.org/whl/torch-2.1.0+cu118.html
```

After a successful installation, you can verify it by importing the library in Python:

```
import torch
import torch_geometric

print(f"PyTorch version: {torch.__version__}")
print(f"PyTorch Geometric version: \
{torch_geometric.__version__}")
```

If this code runs without errors and prints the version numbers, your installation is complete and correct.

B.2 Creating a Basic Graph in PyG

In PyG, a single graph is represented by an instance of the `torch_geometric.data.Data` class. This class is a container for all the properties of your graph. Let's explore its most important attributes:

- **data.x:** The node feature matrix, a tensor of shape **[num_nodes, num_node_features]**. Each row corresponds to a node, and each column corresponds to a feature.
- **data.edge_index:** The graph's connectivity in Coordinate (COO) format. This is a tensor of shape **[2, num_edges]** where the first row contains the source nodes of each edge and the second row contains the target nodes. It's a highly efficient format for sparse matrices.
- **data.edge_attr:** Edge features, a tensor of **shape [num_edges, num_edge_features]**. This is optional and used when edges themselves have attributes (e.g., weights or types).
- **data.y:** The target labels for the graph. Its shape depends on the task. For node-level tasks like node classification, it would be a tensor of shape **[num_nodes]**. For graph-level tasks, it would be a tensor of shape **[1]**.

Let's create a simple, undirected graph with four nodes and five unique edges. Each node will have a 2-dimensional feature vector.

```
import torch
from torch_geometric.data import Data

'''

Define the edges in COO format
 An undirected edge (0, 1) is represented as two
directed edges: (0, 1) and (1, 0)
'''

edge_index = torch.tensor([
    [0, 1, 1, 2, 2, 3, 0, 3],  # Source nodes
    [1, 0, 2, 1, 3, 2, 3, 0]   # Target nodes
], dtype=torch.long)
```

```
# Define node features
# 4 nodes, each with 2 features
x = torch.tensor([
    [-1, 1],  # Features for Node 0
    [1, -1], # Features for Node 1
    [1, 1],  # Features for Node 2
    [-1,-1]  # Features for Node 3
], dtype=torch.float)

# Create the Data object
graph_data = Data(x=x, edge_index=edge_index)
print(graph_data)
```

Running this code will produce the following output:

```
Data(x=[4, 2], edge_index=[2, 8])
```

This summary tells us that our graph_data object represents a graph with 4 nodes (each with 2 features) and 8 edges (4 undirected edges become 8 directed edges). PyG automatically infers the number of nodes from the shape of the x tensor. Notice that we created an undirected graph by explicitly defining edges in both directions (e.g., from node 0 to 1 and from node 1 to 0). This is the standard convention in PyG for representing undirected graphs.

B.3 Basic Operations and Attributes of a Graph

The Data object comes with several useful attributes and methods for inspecting the graph. Let's continue with the `graph_data` object we created earlier.

```
# Get the number of nodes
print(f"Number of nodes: {graph_data.num_nodes}")

# Get the number of edges
print(f"Number of edges: {graph_data.num_edges}")
```

```
# Get the number of node features

print(f"Number of node features: "
f"{graph_data.num_node_features}")

# Check if the graph is undirected

print(f"Is the graph undirected? "
        f"{graph_data.is_undirected()}")
```

The output will be:

```
Number of nodes: 4
Number of edges: 8
Number of node features: 2
Is the graph undirected? True
```

B.3.1 Adding Labels and Masks

For most machine learning tasks, especially semi-supervised node classification, we need to associate labels with our nodes. We also need to define which nodes to use for training, validation, and testing. This is typically done using Boolean masks. Let's add labels and masks to our graph_data object. We can add arbitrary attributes to the Data object by simply assigning them.

```
# Node labels (e.g., for a 2-class classification
problem)
y = torch.tensor([0, 1, 0, 1], dtype=torch.long)

# Create boolean masks for training, validation, and
test sets
train_mask = torch.tensor([True, True, False,
False],
  dtype=torch.bool)
val_mask = torch.tensor([False, False, True, False],
```

```
dtype=torch.bool)
test_mask = torch.tensor([False, False, False,
True],
dtype=torch.bool)

# Add them to our Data object
graph_data.y = y
graph_data.train_mask = train_mask
graph_data.val_mask = val_mask
graph_data.test_mask = test_mask

print(graph_data)
```

The new output will show the added attributes:

```
Data(x=[4, 2], edge_index=[2, 8], y=[4],
 train_mask=[4], val_mask=[4], test_mask=[4])
```

Now our graph data is fully prepared. It contains the graph structure (edge_index), node features (x), ground-truth labels (y), and the necessary masks to partition our data for a standard GNN training workflow.

B.3.2 Modifying a Graph: Adding Nodes and Edges

While Data objects are often treated as immutable once created, you can modify them. Let's add a new edge and a new node to our graph.

Adding a new edge: To add an edge between existing nodes (e.g., between node 0 and node 2), we create a tensor for the new edge and concatenate it with the existing `edge_index`.

```
# New edge from node 0 to 2 (and 2 to 0 for
undirected)
new_edge=torch.tensor([[0,2],[2,0]],dtype=torch.
long)
```

```
graph_data.edge_index = torch.cat([graph_data.
edge_index,\
 new_edge], dim=1)

print(f"Edges after adding new edge:"
 f"{graph_data.edge_index}")
print(f"Number of edges after adding:"
 f"{graph_data.num_edges}")
```

Adding a new node: Adding a new node requires updating all node-level attributes. Let's add a fifth node (index 4) and connect it to node 1.

```
# 1. Add features for the new node

# Features for node 4
new_node_features = torch.tensor([[0, 0]],\
 dtype=torch.float)
graph_data.x = torch.cat([graph_data.x,\
 new_node_features], dim=0)
# 2. Add an edge from new node 4 to existing node 1
new_edge_to_new_node = torch.tensor([[1, 4], [4,
1]],\
 dtype=torch.long)
graph_data.edge_index = torch.cat([graph_data.
edge_index,\
 new_edge_to_new_node], dim=1)

# 3. Update labels and masks for the new node
graph_data.y = torch.cat([graph_data.y, torch.
tensor([0],\
 dtype=torch.long)], dim=0) # Assign label 0
graph_data.train_mask = torch.cat([graph_data.
train_mask, torch.tensor([False], dtype=torch.bool)],
dim=0)
graph_data.val_mask = torch.cat([graph_data.val_mask,\
 torch.tensor([False], dtype=torch.bool)], dim=0)
 # Put new node in test set
graph_data.test_mask = torch.cat([graph_data.
test_mask,\
```

```
   torch.tensor([True], dtype=torch.bool)], dim=0)

  print("\n--- After Adding New Node ---")
  print(graph_data)
```

After these operations, the final graph_data object will have 5 nodes and 12 edges (8 original + 2 new + 2 to the new node).

Its summary will be:

```
Data(x=[5, 2], edge_index=[2, 12], y=[5],\
 train_mask=[5], val_mask=[5], test_mask=[5])
```

B.4 Loading Existing Datasets

Manually creating Data objects is useful for understanding the structure, but in practice, we often work with existing benchmark datasets. PyG provides easy access to a wide variety of these through the torch_geometric.datasets module. Let's load the popular Cora dataset, a citation network where nodes are scientific publications and edges are citations between them. The task is to classify each publication into one of several topics.

```
from torch_geometric.datasets import Planetoid

'''
Load the Cora dataset
The dataset will be downloaded to the specified
'root' directory the first time.
'''

dataset = Planetoid(root='/tmp/Cora', name='Cora')

print(f"Dataset: {dataset}")
print(f"Number of graphs: {len(dataset)}")
```

```
print(f"Number of features: {dataset.num_features}")
print(f"Number of classes: {dataset.num_classes}")
```

The output will look like this:

```
Dataset: Cora()
Number of graphs: 1
Number of features: 1433
Number of classes: 7
```

The Cora dataset, like many node classification benchmarks in PyG, is represented as a single graph. We can access this graph's Data object directly. It's common practice to place the entire dataset on a single variable for convenience.

```
# Get the first (and only) graph object from the
dataset
data = dataset[0]

print("\nGraph data object:")
print(data)
```

This will print a summary of the Data object for the Cora graph:

```
Graph data object:
Data(x=[2708, 1433], edge_index=[2, 10556], y=[2708],\
 train_mask=[2708], val_mask=[2708], test_mask=[2708])
```

This tells us that the Cora graph has 2,708 nodes (publications), each with a 1,433-dimensional feature vector (a bag-of-words representation of the paper's text). It has 10,556 edges (citations). Crucially, the dataset comes pre-loaded with train_mask, val_mask, and test_mask, which specify the standard splits for training, validation, and testing, as established in the original research papers.

B.5 Accelerating with a GPU

For large graphs and complex models, training on a CPU can be slow. PyTorch and PyG make it simple to switch to a GPU (like an NVIDIA GPU with CUDA support) for a significant speed-up. The standard practice is to define a device and move both the model and the data to it.

```
'''
Check if a CUDA-enabled GPU is available,
 otherwise fall back to CPU
'''

device = torch.device('cuda' if torch.cuda.
is_available()\
                      else 'cpu')

print(f"Using device: {device}")

# Move the data to the chosen device
data = data.to(device)
```

From this point on, all computations involving the data object will be performed on the selected device. We must also ensure our model is on the same device.

B.6 Defining a GNN Architecture

Now we will define a simple Graph Neural Network model using PyG's layers. We will build a two-layer Graph Convolutional Network (GCN). The process is identical to building a standard neural network in PyTorch: we create a class that inherits from torch.nn.Module.

PyG's torch_geometric.nn module contains a rich library of GNN layers. We will use GCNConv.

```
import torch.nn.functional as F
from torch_geometric.nn import GCNConv
```

```
class GCN(torch.nn.Module):
    def __init__(self, num_node_features, num_classes):
        super(GCN, self).__init__()
        '''First GCN layer: maps node features to a
        16-dimensional hidden space'''
        self.conv1 = GCNConv(num_node_features, 16)
        '''Second GCN layer: maps 16-dim hidden space
to
        the number of classes'''
        self.conv2 = GCNConv(16, num_classes)

    def forward(self, data):
        # data object contains the full graph
        x, edge_index = data.x, data.edge_index

        # 1 First GCN layer + ReLU activation
        x = self.conv1(x, edge_index)
        x = F.relu(x)

        # 2 Optional: Dropout for regularization
        x = F.dropout(x, training=self.training)

        # 3 Second GCN layer
        x = self.conv2(x, edge_index)

        ''' 4. Output raw scores (logits) for each
class.
         A softmax function will be applied later in
         the loss function.
         '''
        return x

''' Let's instantiate the model using the parameters
    from our Cora dataset
'''
model = GCN(num_node_features=dataset.num_features,\
            num_classes=dataset.num_classes).to(device)
print(model)

print(model)
```

The output shows the architecture of our model:

```
GCN(
  (conv1): GCNConv(1433, 16)
  (conv2): GCNConv(16, 7)
)
```

Our forward method defines the computation at each forward pass. It takes the data object, unpacks the node features x and the graph structure edge_index, and passes them through the GCN layers. The first layer computes hidden embeddings for each node, and the second layer computes the final output logits for classification.

B.7 Training the GNN

Finally, we'll write the training loop to optimize our model's parameters. This follows a standard PyTorch training pattern.

First, we set up our optimizer (we'll use Adam) and the loss function. For multi-class classification, CrossEntropyLoss is the standard choice.

```
# Set up optimizer
optimizer = torch.optim.Adam(model.parameters(),\
lr=0.01,weight_decay=5e-4)
# Set up loss function
criterion = torch.nn.CrossEntropyLoss()
```

Now, we create the training loop. In each epoch, we perform a forward pass, calculate the loss only on the training nodes (using data.train_mask), and update the model's weights.

```
def train():
    model.train() # Set the model to training mode
    optimizer.zero_grad() # Clear gradients
```

```
    # Perform a single forward pass
    out = model(data)

    # Calculate loss only on training nodes
    loss = criterion(out[data.train_mask],\
                     data.y[data.train_mask])

    # Backpropagate and update weights
    loss.backward()
    optimizer.step()
    return loss

def test():
    model.eval() # Set the model to evaluation mode
    out = model(data)
    # Use the class with highest probability.
    pred = out.argmax(dim=1)

    # Calculate accuracy on the test set
    test_correct = pred[data.test_mask] ==\
                        data.y[data.test_mask]
    test_acc = int(test_correct.sum()) / \
               int(data.test_mask.sum())
    return test_acc

# Training loop
for epoch in range(1, 201):
    loss = train()
    if epoch % 10 == 0:
      print(f'Epoch: {epoch:03d}, Loss: {loss:.4f}')

# Final evaluation on the test set
test_accuracy = test()
print(f'Test Accuracy: {test_accuracy:.4f}')
```

In this loop, the `train()` function handles one epoch of training. The key step is `criterion(out[data.`

`train_mask], data.y[data.train_mask])`. Here, we use the train_mask to select the model's predictions and the ground-truth labels for only the nodes in the training set. This ensures that the model learns only from the training data. The `test()` function evaluates the model's performance. It sets the model to evaluation mode (disabling dropout) and calculates the classification accuracy on the held-out test set, again using the appropriate mask (test_mask). After 200 epochs, you can expect to see a test accuracy of around 80% or higher on the Cora dataset with this simple GCN model.

This appendix has provided a foundational introduction to the PyTorch Geometric library, covering the essential steps from installation and graph creation to model training and evaluation. While we have focused on a basic GCN architecture for node classification, the principles demonstrated here serve as a launchpad for exploring more complex models and tasks. Throughout the book, you will find numerous programming assignments, accessible via online resources, that delve into different GNN architectures and applications. We strongly encourage readers to engage with these hands-on exercises to solidify their understanding and build practical skills in graph machine learning.

References

Ahmed, A., Shervashidze, N., Narayanamurthy, S., Josifovski, V., & Smola, A. J. (2013). Distributed large-scale natural graph factorization. In *Proceedings of the 22nd International World Wide Web Conference* (pp. 37–48).

Bishop, C. M. (2006). *Pattern recognition and machine learning*. Springer.

Cao, S., Lu, W., & Xu, Q. (2015). GraRep: Learning graph representations with global structural information. In *Proceedings of the 24th ACM International Conference on Information and Knowledge Management* (pp. 891–900).

Chen, J., Ma, T., & Xiao, C. (2018). FastGCN: Fast learning with graph convolutional networks via importance sampling. In *Proceedings of the 6th International Conference on Learning Representations* (ICLR).

Chiang, W.-L., Liu, X., Si, S., Li, Y., Bengio, S., & Hsieh, C.-J. (2019). Cluster-GCN: An efficient algorithm for training deep and large graph convolutional networks. In *Proceedings of the 25th ACM SIGKDD International Conference on Knowledge Discovery and Data Mining* (pp. 257–266).

Friedberg, S. H., Insel, A. J., & Spence, L. E. (2013). *Linear algebra* (Pearson new international ed.). Pearson Higher Education.

Goodfellow, I., Bengio, Y., & Courville, A. (2016). *Deep learning*. MIT Press. http://www.deeplearningbook.org

Grover, A., & Leskovec, J. (2016). node2vec: Scalable feature learning for networks. In *Proceedings of the 22nd ACM SIGKDD International Conference on Knowledge Discovery and Data Mining* (pp. 855–864).

Hamilton, W. L., Ying, Z., & Leskovec, J. (2017). Inductive representation learning on large graphs. In *Advances in Neural Information Processing Systems* (Vol. 30).

Kipf, T. N., & Welling, M. (2016). Variational graph auto-encoders. *arXiv*. https://arxiv.org/abs/1611.07308

Lee, J., Lee, I., & Kang, J. (2019). Self-attention graph pooling. In *Proceedings of the 36th International Conference on Machine Learning* (pp. 3734–3743). PMLR.

Li, Y., Tarlow, D., Brockschmidt, M., & Zemel, R. (2016). Gated graph sequence neural networks. *arXiv.* https://arxiv.org/abs/1511.05493

Liben-Nowell, D., & Kleinberg, J. (2003). The link prediction problem for social networks. In *Proceedings of the 12th International Conference on Information and Knowledge Management* (pp. 556–559).

Montesinos López, O. A., Montesinos López, A., & Crossa, J. (2022). Overfitting, model tuning, and evaluation of prediction performance. In *Multivariate statistical machine learning methods for genomic prediction* (Chap. 4). Springer.

Perozzi, B., Al-Rfou, R., & Skiena, S. (2014). DeepWalk: Online learning of social representations. In *Proceedings of the 20th ACM SIGKDD International Conference on Knowledge Discovery and Data Mining* (pp. 701–710).

Selsam, D., Lamm, M., Bünz, B., Liang, P., de Moura, L., & Dill, D. L. (2019). Learning a SAT solver from single-bit supervision. In *Proceedings of the 7th International Conference on Learning Representations* (ICLR).

Veličković, P., Cucurull, G., Casanova, A., Romero, A., Liò, P., & Bengio, Y. (2018). Graph attention networks. In *Proceedings of the 6th International Conference on Learning Representations* (ICLR).

Wang, M., Yu, L., Zheng, D., Gan, Q., Gai, Y., Ye, Z., … Zhang, Z. (2019). Deep graph library: Towards efficient and scalable deep learning on graphs. In *ICLR Workshop on Representation Learning on Graphs and Manifolds.*

Wang, S., Hu, L., Wang, Y., He, X., Sheng, Q. Z., Orgun, M. A., & Yu, P. S. (2021). Graph learning–based recommender systems: A review. *arXiv.* https://arxiv.org/abs/2105.06339

Xu, K., Li, C., Tian, Y., Sonobe, T., Kawarabayashi, K., & Jegelka, S. (2018). Representation learning on graphs with jumping knowledge networks. In *Proceedings of the 35th International Conference on Machine Learning* (pp. 5453–5462). PMLR.

Zeng, H., Zhou, H., Srivastava, A., Kannan, R., & Prasanna, V. (2020). GraphSAINT: Graph sampling based inductive learning method. In *Proceedings of the 8th International Conference on Learning Representations* (ICLR).

Zhang, A., Lipton, Z. C., Li, M., & Smola, A. J. (2023). *Dive into deep learning*. Cambridge University Press. https://d2l.ai

Zhang, M., & Chen, Y. (2018). Link prediction based on graph neural networks. In *Advances in Neural Information Processing Systems* (Vol. 31).

Zheng, D., Song, X., Ma, C., Tan, Z., Ye, Z., Dong, H., … Zhang, Z. (2020). DistDGL: Distributed graph neural network training for billion-scale graphs. *arXiv*. https://arxiv.org/abs/2010.05337

www.ingramcontent.com/pod-product-compliance
Lightning Source LLC
LaVergne TN
LVHW022213200926
848481LV00006B/1946
* 9 7 8 1 6 3 6 5 1 7 2 5 4 *